SQUIRT BOATING & BEYOND:
How to Rip in Anything that Squirts

WRITTEN BY
James E. Snyder

ILLUSTRATED BY
William Nealy

SQUIRT BOATING & BEYOND:
How to Rip in Anything that Squirts

MENASHA RIDGE PRESS
Birmingham, Alabama

Printed in the United States of America
Published by Menasha Ridge Press
Distributed by The Globe Pequot Press
First edition, first printing

Library of Congress Cataloging-in-Publication Data

Snyder, James E., 1954-
Squirt boating and beyond: how to rip in anything
that squirts / by James E. Snyder;
illustrated by William Nealy.

p. cm.
Includes index.

ISBN 0-89732-373-4 (alk. paper)

1. White-water canoeing. 2. Kayaking. I. Nealy,
William, 1953- II. Title.

GV788 .S68 2001
797.1'224--dc21

Photography by Paul Marshall and Kevin O'Brien

Cover photograph by James E. Snyder

Cover and text design by Grant M. Tatum

Menasha Ridge Press
P.O. Box 43673
Birmingham, AL 35243
www.menasharidge.com

GOD IS A JEWEL CUTTER

He turns us round an' roun'
to let his light go deep within
and show our inner flaws
which craze the light
and split the night
as nothing will again.
Then some careful cuts are made
to show some unseen plan.
At last he holds us high and far
and smiles while he can;
admiring how we dance with light—
when once were only sand ...

—Jim Snyder

DEDICATION

This book is dedicated to my family and friends—past, present, and future. Without their dedication, I would have never found the Champagne World, nor my wings. We need to remember our departed friends because they add to our lives and are appreciated. They make us grateful, and gratitude is the number one attitude. Our family reminds us that this *is* life or death and it **does** matter. My family and friends are good for my heart and my heart is good for my life. So these ties are key.

The book is also dedicated to "fun." It's a wispy concept—not necessarily trouble-free. But it is educational and worthwhile. Properly pursued, it is inspiring. It's like a thread of intent which finds its way through the hazards and distractions. I wish everyone cool curvy charcs.

SPECIAL THANKS

To William Nealy, the co-creator of this book. Based on a handful of text, a lot of instinct, and a half hour of video, he learned the feel of every new squirt move—pencil first! I understand he had a little model buddy to help him get a lot of the perspective in order, but his knowledge of the moves comes through crystal-clear in the illustrations. I feel he raised his talent a notch to meet this challenge like no one else in the world could. We are all thankful for the supreme effort and attention to detail he included in every depiction. He rendered the instant and surreal into frozen and real for us.

To Bill Friend, who helped me start my design career. I had a wood-strip plug of my first design—the Slice—in the spring of 1980, and I was approaching the finishing stages (I thought) and wasn't sure how to proceed. I ended up talking to him one day about how I believed that 4-meter boats would be better if they were shorter, and how I was working on a 10' 4" "playboat." He agreed with the concept and volunteered to help. When he finally saw the plug, it was not what he had expected or preferred—but he still spent a week in the hot sun, sanding and helping me through the final shaping and polishing stages. He then molded this big, fat, cigar-looking Slice, and we pulled my first boat from it shortly after. A few months later, I showed it to Vladmir Vanha and asked him if he would like to build them for sale. He said, "Maybe YOU should build MY designs. I have been thinking of doing something similar but handling the lines a little more ... delicately." He was right, and he went on to start the successful line of "spud" boats he's now famous for. Bill Friend helped me for free—because it was something he believed in. He did it to help make a funner thing for everybody. He did it ... for Freedom. He was one of the old school hot dogs at that time—guys like Jimmy Stuart, Jimmy Holcombe, and Tom Irwin. No one hardly remembers these guys. And these guys don't care, because they are still having fun. Squirtsport is a mutant child of their playful intentions way, way, back in the murky depths of time. So kudos also to the ancient amphibians. Their charc is not lost.

TABLE OF CONTENTS

SQUIRT BOATING & BEYOND:
How to Rip in Anything that Squirts

FOREWORD

When I first met the young, raw Jim Snyder, I immediately sensed his great potential and urged him to spend a year in Hamburg, Germany, perfecting his craft. Oh, I'm sorry. That was the advice I gave The Beatles.

Stephen King was originally slated to write this foreword, but that fell through when Jim Snyder realized he didn't know Stephen King. I think King would have made it much too scary, anyway. I don't like a scary foreword myself and believe me, I like rabid dogs and dismembered bodies as much as anybody.

The reason I have been chosen to pen this intro is because I don't squirt now and indeed have never squirted. Don't get me wrong. I've done some amazing things in my life. I've parachuted out of a plane, played tennis with Rod Laver, and had breakfast with Jimi Hendrix.

But I've never been in a squirt boat, and Snyder knows how cool I think his sport is. The boats rock. Mystery Moves? If it'll help me escape my creditors even for a few seconds, I want in. All the secrets of squirt boating are in these pages, and Jim Snyder knows them all. All you need is a river and this book, and within a matter of weeks you'll be able to parallel park inside a whirlpool and do-si-do with your paddle.

And you'll look sharp, too. I'm wearing a spray skirt right now, and trust me, I've never looked more stunning.

—Barry Friedman, Valencia, California

PREFACE

Charc in equals charc out—times *variables*. And these variables are where the history of the mystery resides. These variables are the blend of the infinite detail and the perfect flaw. They are what lead us where we've never been. The variables are ever-present and exist on the horizon with ambiguity, indecision, . . . and magic. They are the river's way of talking to us and teaching us. Our interaction with the river can be perceived as a conversation of action. And, as in most conversations, the outcome is a question of style. You have a unique style. But the river keeps hammering and cajoling it into a better form. Your relationship with the river is an endless continuum of evolution and you must find your pace somehow. Once your pace is found, *everything* is a question of style—even the variables—even the magic.

So what can I tell you about this . . . style? Nothing. I don't want you to be any different and if you were to become "better," what good would it do? The answer escapes me. But I suggest you do what you can to leave your baggage on shore and lighten up and play a bit. Float for the joy of it. There is so much the river offers in its simplicity and each reward seems customized. It *must* be magic. Are you ready for that? It's your destiny, and how you relate to joy is a question of style. If you are to be liberated, you must be ready for the consequences. Many players arrest their progress because they can't answer the question, "What's next?" And so, many play on the temple steps, but few enter. To attain oneness with funness is inspiring.

Don't look here to hone your style. This book is only a tool and a touchstone. Use it to map where you can go and to find the way to power up your charc. This way is clearly through the basics—your "stations." Your stations are a moment of poise as you perch over the end of your boat. No matter if you strive to purée a perfect hole into a fish frappé or just sublimely slide into the Netherlands of the underworld, your only glimpse of control is through the windows of your stations. If you're not checking your stations, you're getting lost. If you are getting lost, you are flirting with "oblivion charcs" and you won't get there. You will find yourself human and fall short of amphibian status. You want style? You want stations.

Perhaps rodeo boaters will find this book in a search for

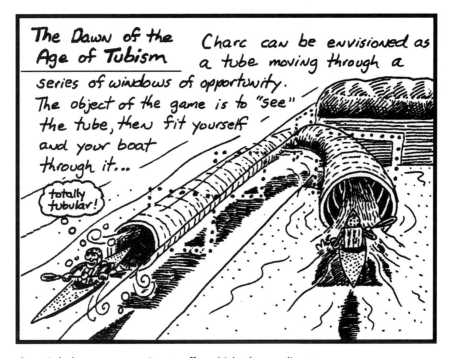

clues. I do have a suggestion to offer which also applies to squirt boaters. **Good form** is the path to higher energy scenarios. Think of it as valences of energy. You can't make it to the higher levels of energy without a good solid base in the level below. And then you must explore the upper level before you can master it. Upper levels of dynamic interaction are realms of harmony and serendipity. They are a way of agreeing with your environment. They are a blending of wills. To find this realm you need some intangible tools—appetite and tenacity. These tools have nothing to do with ambition or glory, so give up on that. They are born of amphibious yearnings. I think it might be genetic. You could be a merson, a "mer"-person. So don't deny these yearnings. Fulfill them.

What if you find yourself truly amphibious? What could it mean to anyone? It's only meaningful to you. And what it means is Life is Short. I won't tell you to live every minute as if it were your last. I won't tell you that mellow is groovy either. But I will say that life can be wild beyond your imagination. And to find this realm—**beyond**—you must be hungry for it and you must hold to your path with determination. Appetite and tenacity. You can take that from this book perhaps. I hope it serves you well.

3

ACKNOWLEDGMENTS

I'd like to acknowledge William Nealy's phenomenal work in this book. He has cubically liberated the text. I also want to thank Paul Marshall for his photographs and friendship. And finally, I'd like to thank all the old-time squirt boaters who have proven you can do this sort of thing for decades and stay inspired. I hope this sport brings the "deepest" satisfaction to anyone searching for buried pleasures. Seek a sweet charc—and find it!

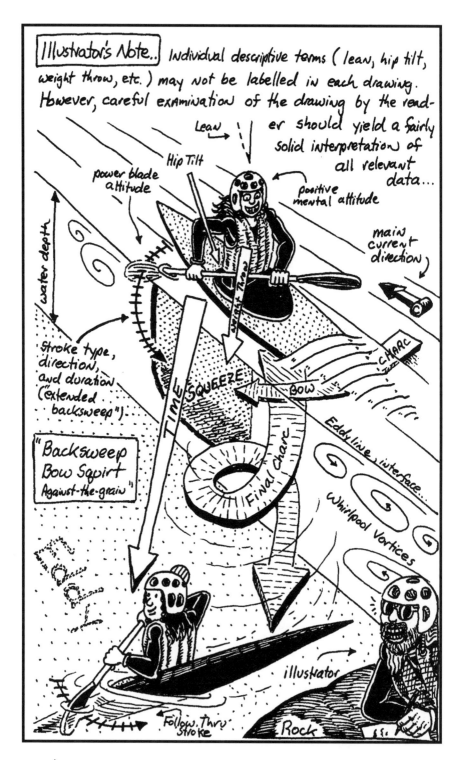

6

INTRODUCTION
The Origins of Squirtech

Squirtech had its beginnings in the slalom-racing corner of the sport. Fierce competition finally gave racers the nerve to lean their boats the **wrong** way in a turn. The success of the move is now history, but it was hard to accept at the time. The best racers were making their best efforts, and so began the squirt tradition of limits being redefined. Thanks to this cumulative effort, squirtists will never **master** their sport. In fact, we all can say that we are just learning. This humble legacy is truly a privilege to share. Squirtists should reflect on the spirit revealed in the history of our subsport. It is indomitable and inimitable, a rock in time, a stroke for all. It is the one point central to all squirt development.

This spirit is a thing in itself and uses us to become real. We are lucky to be along for the ride. My mind runs back a few years to a foggy morning on the Savage River. The spirit was there. Jimmy Stuart, a man who performed perhaps the first Ender in America, came screaming through the fog. Launching off a wave, he landed next to me in an eddy. A friend, noticing his sparkling style, said, "Stuart, you are unreal." As he cruised back into the froth, I could hear him say, "Naw, I'm surreal." The spirit originates in all of us and allows us to become more. Being a squirtist means partici- pating in the evolution of freedom. I hope to communicate to you the spirit I see in the squirtists I know. The following is a history of squirting as I've experienced it. I can't cover the contributions of everyone involved, but I feel I've included the key happenings and people. I apologize for anyone unrecognized, but I realize the entire progress of squirting has been accomplished for one reason alone, the ride. Let me say then that if you didn't get a mention, you at least have your ride. And that should be enough.

Early History

The first attempt at the squirt concept that I ever saw worked. Eric Evans was the man, and the 1970 National Slalom Championships on the West River in Vermont was the setting. Course designers wanted racers to tediously run a down- stream gate on the river left side of a rock, eddy up, and peel out the river right side to catch the next downstream gate. Eric was a victim of his realm of superior speed and could not travel the beaten path. Instead, he threaded a

Lean Comparisons...

Inside Lean

Outside Lean

Motorcycle

Squirt Boat

straight line across the river and through the gates. Besides running close tolerances, he had to perform a radical lean into the currents of the eddy. Leaning to the outside of the turn, opposite the way a motorcycle leans, required that he do some strong strokes on the downstream side in the eddy for support. He went very fast and cleaned both gates. He found that rebounding off currents produces a faster reaction than merely blending with their surfaces. Effective and flashy, the move became the wave of the future, even though no one else tried it that day. Over the next ten years, it became quite established and was a key factor in the rush to cut volume out of race boats. Winning races these days has a lot to do with how effectively you do your squirts. So, though the move has been swallowed by the realm of fun, science should get the credit for its parentage.

America's world class C-1 paddlers from the Washington D.C. area, David Hearn, Jon Lugbill, and others, were the first folks that I heard had "high" squirts. In the early days, around 1979, a high squirt was about head high. Anything higher than this is useless for racing. Thank goodness those guys were into having fun too. They have had a lot to do with the rebonding of the cruising and racing factions of this sport. Experts in both realms, they give everybody someone to look up to. In these early days, someone in the D.C. area named the move "Pivot Turns." The name has stuck in that region; now you can tell what school squirtists come from by how they name the move.

Phil Coleman, an ancient expert kayaker/raft guide from the Upper Yough area, developed the move on his own during the same era. It was he who dubbed the move "squirt." When he would describe the move to people who had never heard of it, he would point out how the boat squeezes out of the water, accelerating forward as it returns to the surface. This is the quality of value to racers. He said it was like a bar of soap squirting out of your hands. The name came to him at the top of Tear Drop Rapid in the Cheat River Canyon. He squirted out of an eddy at the top of the last big drop and was propelled into the rapid at pumpkin-seed speed. The name seemed so right we had no choice but to accept it.

These two areas were the original hotbeds of the squirt world. From racing, I believe, the move quickly spread to the Southern C-1ers. These boaters have traditionally been among the best in the country. They had no trouble becoming quite proficient at it. From these areas, the move spread by word of mouth, friend to friend, to California, Maine, Oregon, and even St. Louis and New Mexico. Aggressive young experts answered the call. This subsport has always been considered radical, and as such has had a limited appeal, basically to the lunatic fringe.

Modern-day three-dimensionology has gone far beyond the horizons set by its early pioneers. This is due largely to a catalytic character by the name of Jesse Whittemore. His timely influence on the sport cannot be overestimated. My brother Jeff and I were lucky to be present that winter of 1981 in Albright, West Virginia, when Jesse got a burr under his saddle. Jesse had moved there from the Baltimore area to work for Cheat River Outfitters, a local rafting outfit. The three of us made a habit of paddling almost every day that winter. Jeff and I were there to perfect our backsurfing and paddle throwing, while Jesse was in it just for the kicks. The chopped race boat he paddled was dangerously small for his large-framed body. It seemed that he could only keep one end of it afloat at any one time. Over and over, Jesse would break out of an eddy and sink his upstream hip and then his stern. He became quite skilled at head-high squirts. We watched spellbound as his squirts attained higher and higher limits. In a couple of short, cold months, he was performing perfect Backenders on eddy lines. It really looked like fun. Before long, it seemed we were going boating to watch

Jesse. We knew that we had to get into the act before we fossilized.

As Jesse's boat seemed too big for me to squirt, I decided to come up with one of my own. I decided to chop a Slice, a short cruising boat that Bill Friend and I had created a couple of years before. In spring of 1982, with the help of John Regan and Danger Bob, I chopped the Slice and made the Trice. John is a well-known expert and Bob is a well-known beginner. We all thought the Trice was pretty hot stuff. It was small, surfed very nicely, and could do Backender squirts. The Trice was the beginning of a blitz of squirt boat designs by myself in an effort to combine high performance with passable comfort. Before Gauley season that year, I modified the Trice by making it longer with a flat deck and a W-shaped hull. The Forth was an interesting but inconclusive design. It was hard to say if the W helped or not. By Gauley season, I had filled in the W, which created the Bounty.

In the meantime, Jesse modified his race boat, adding canards to the bow (wing-like structures) and modifying the hull some. The new boat became a classic success, the Millenium Falcon. Jesse kept improving his skills and was generally considered the best squirtist on water. He proved his edge by founding one of the most noteworthy and daring moves in the sport, the Rock Splat. He would maneuver his boat to the upstream side of a rock and balance there sideways. When he felt the time was right, he would lean the boat upstream and pry it to vertical. There he would perch, a couple of inches from the rock, surfing its pillow. It was pretty scary to watch, but he was usually in control. He said he discovered the move one day that summer when he was feeling out the currents on the upstream side of a rock in one of the last rapids on the Lower Yough. He noticed how they kept tugging at his hip, trying to flip him over upstream. Always open to new tricks, he said, "Fine, take me." The resulting move was his alone for several months while everyone tried to build up the nerve and skill to match him.

After Gauley season, I decided my squirt boat should be more surfboard-like, with a fuller top profile than the pointy Bounty. I widened the bow and flattened the hull, creating the Bound To. I made only one because it was enough to convince me to start from scratch to attain a very surfboard-like design. In fact, many people thought the resulting design was a hollowed-out surfboard.

The Baby Arc is Born

In January 1983, the baby Arc was born. At twenty-four gallons volume, it was the most radical squirt design ever. The plug was built from twelve two-inch-thick poplar boards, sawn to the boat's sideview profile. I nailed and glued them together to form a ten-by-two-foot cutting board. I used a chainsaw and cut through nails and all to establish the top-view profile. Two days of grinding later, the shape was there. A thin coat of putty for a finish and the tiny plug was done, weighing in at a mere 120 pounds. There was only one ever built, but it was in this design that I accomplished the first flatwater Cartwheels (about 12 ends). After I discovered it was really too small for me but perfect for my brother Jeff, he became the sole owner. I made a slightly scaled-up version for myself. The spring 1983 floods were the format for the proving of the "dense-boat theory." In very big water, the small Arcs proved able to deliver a steady and superior ride. Punching eight-foot holes became quite fun with a boat that penetrated through as level as it entered. We also accomplished the first Screw Ups and Cartwheels in these boats that spring. These are fun moves, described later in detail, and were early steps to the total access modes we now use. Jeff and I worked as a team to polish our techniques on these.

In late spring, Jeff had an unfortunate accident on the Big Sandy River in West Virginia, at the Bridge Pier Rapid. He turned out of an eddy on a squirt, when his stern was held fast to a rock underwater. As the boat folded down, succumbing to fierce green currents, the bow hit another rock. The deep, unyielding currents caused the boat to buckle at a weak point between his knees and feet. My brother traded a mangled left leg and a greenstick fracture (bones partly broken, partly bent) of the tibia and fibula bones of his right leg for a sure drowning death. He rolled up just upstream of a fallen tree with his bow bent skyward, creased in all the wrong places. He made it to shore above the tree but went into minor shock as we removed his limp legs from the tiny boat. We splinted him with sticks and string and carefully put him into a Riverchaser with the front wall removed. It was a hard realization that he had to paddle out the last two miles of Class IV whitewater, but any other evacuation would have been even more difficult and time-consuming. Jeff had a painful run and seemed to be on the verge of passing out at times. We loaded him—still in the kayak—into a truck. It took over four hours to get him to the hospital, plenty of time for his shock to wear off, which sent him even deeper into his realm of pain. At the hospital, they cut his wetsuit, reinforced his anatomy with rust-less hardware, and, worst of all, plastered his leg so fat it wouldn't fit in his Arc. Looking back now, I'm sure his greatest regrets, though, concerned the six weeks of boating he missed. Jeff said the lesson for all was never to make a move without a plan. Oblivion charcs always leave you short of your goal because oblivion, by its very nature, is unattainable.

In June 1983, in an effort to improve my Arc 2, I designed the Arc 3. I started with a foam blank and added putty to establish more rocker and foot room. It was a fine boat and several people own copies. It was a hot surfer and could do Cartwheels. That summer, Phoenix, a production kayak manufacturer from Berea, Kentucky, got the first jump on the production squirt boat market by buying the rights to the Arc. I spent the fall developing the Arcs 4, 5, and 6, the latter being the best and the one Phoenix used. In November, John Regan, Greg Green, Jeff, and I ran the Grand Canyon

at 27,000 cfs in our squirt boats. We rode whirlpools that were thirty feet around with two-foot cores. All you could see was the top one foot of the rider's bow as he would swirl in the core with a cone of air reaching his lungs. This provided an unusual toilet's-eye-view of the world. In his baby Arc, Jeff would sometimes be completely swallowed by diagonal folds in the currents. His tiny boat also provided the most stable ride through the huge holes he punched. We all had fantastic rides, including one in which I had a long talk with the Reaper, deep in a whirlpool at the bottom right of Lava Falls. He said any time I wanted to talk to God, I just had to drop in. John went on to be a key member of the Wave Sport company as they were going through their exciting expansion years. His super clean plug work brought a new standard of excellence to the plastic industry. The kayaks he built in the early eighties are valued collector's items, as are Jesse's creations from that era.

Jesse specialized in high-tech lay-ups and truly artful gel coats. Jesse also helped Perception design the Sabre kayak, which met with modest success as a squirt boat but came into its own as an ocean surf kayak a decade later. He got to star in the company's promotional video, "Blasting Into the Third Dimension," and taught many early squirt clinics across America. His manufacturing company, Whittemore Laminates, turned out numerous memorable "long, fast, and pointy" squirt designs like the Cylon and Blaster and a cool short squirt boat named the Cyborg. He wasn't well poised for expansion, however, and his production ground to a halt in the late eighties. He later went on to play a pivotal role in the development of Mountain Surf, a notable high quality accessories company, in the nineties. He also became quite involved in the local race scene and became a significant competitor to reckon with.

Meanwhile, Jesse negotiated the acquisition of the Sabre Kayak manufacturing company. This was owned by our friends, the Peppers, and had been previously maintained by John Brown—one of the best-known, super-high-quality kayak builders ever.

In the late summer of 1984, I designed the Special Production Arc, or Sparc. I flattened the decks of the Arc 6 to better its Cartwheel ability. It worked, but my plug work was a little crude, due in part to the fact that I did the plug work in the woods, with only a platform for a shop. In an effort to clean up my lines and reduce the boat to the minimum volume necessary, I designed the Ride that December. It was a dandy little boat, with the emphasis on little. Unlimited in its Cartwheel potential, the boat also had tons of rocker but was a little tippy. By suggestion of Bob Taylor of Farmville, Virginia, I widened the Ride to create the Wide Ride in January 1985. This was a very pleasing design featuring a flat bottom and hard chines. It had a distinct seam line that dipped underwater from the hips to the stern. This made it squirt instantly but also left the boat slightly unbalanced between its bow and stern volume. I raised the edge to level with the waterline and rounded the flats of the hull to create a more slippery feel while surfing. The resulting design was called the Plane, the boat in which Jeff and I discovered the Mystery Move.

I was invited to give squirt clinics in the Portland, Oregon, area in the summer of 1985 by my old friend Thom Powell, who runs the River City Kayak School there. I had a great time and was well impressed by the low-key nature of the highly skilled paddlers I met there. I found the basalt bed whitewater somewhat intimidating but managed to keep plenty of air in my lungs. It was Thom who named the Mystery Move. The move involves completely submerging the kayak and rider in an eddy line or whirlpool: literally disappearing. The Sparc and Wide Ride molds are in Thom's care. He rents them to people desiring access to the third dimension.

The Jet Takes Off

On returning from out West, in an effort to make the Plane more comfortable, I went back to the plug and built toe "tunnels" and rounded the hull even more. These tunnels were the original predecessors of the "foot bumps" which would become a dominant feature in squirt and rodeo designs from then on, although the original whitewater kayaks with foot bumps were Klepper kayaks back in the late sixties. So the Plane evolved into the Jet, which became so popular that I was unable to satisfy the demand for them and granted production rights to John Schreiner of New Wave Kayaks. I also let the rights out to a few small other companies at the time, but they were unable to stay in business over the long run. New Wave specialized in custom sizing and graphics and the bulk of their boats were crafted by John's brother Paul. New Wave went on to become the biggest manufacturer of squirt boats in the world until they went out of business in 1999. At that point, Paul took control of the molds and production under his new company, Paul Schreiner Composites.

The summer of 1985 also featured the first Eastern Squirt Championships. They were held on the Black River in Waterton, New York. Jeff won them paddling a Jet.

A truly low point in squirt history occurred in March 1986. Allen Connelly, 24, was paddling a Jet I made for him down the Lower Gauley River at 20,000 cfs. The group had cleaned almost all the tough rapids with Allen rolling two or three times but nevertheless running strong lines. Like everyone else in the group, he eddied up between Upper and Lower Stairstep Rapids, but somewhere in the area of the eddy, his friends lost sight of him. His body was found the next day, still in the boat with his skirt on, washed up on shore. There was only about one gallon of water in his boat. When I inspected the boat later, I found that it had not collapsed or even cracked. Heavy abrasion marks indicated that the boat had been trapped nearly level over two rocks, plugging an underwater drain of sorts. I found deep zigzag scratches where he'd obviously wiggled the boat in an effort to free it. No one will ever know why he didn't escape the boat and swim. There were no body abrasions to indicate a body entrapment. It is also a mystery where his paddle went. Members of the group pointed out the cool spring day and

cold water, and no doubt he was tired. These all must have been factors.

His death caused a reevaluation of intent and recommitment in the squirt sport. He was a fine friend to those who knew him and squirting was a cherished part of his life. Many squirtists have used this lesson to clean up their charcs and, in the long run, knowledge of Al's death may save many lives. Needless to say, it took a lot of wind out of my sails, leaving me with just my boat and friends but no incentive. It made me realize that I am probably a terminal squirtist also, and thus live on borrowed time.

Summer of 1986 saw the first National Squirt Championships, held on the Ocoee River in Tennessee. They were also won by my brother Jeff in his Jet. In fact, the first three places were won by Jetists. This was also the year of the first squirt videos, produced by Rocky Rossi of Gravity Sports Films, featuring Jeff and Jesse, and another produced by my nuclear physicist friend Paul Marshall of Marshall Arts. This was called *Fun Forever* and became a classic. *Fun Forever* features a custom soundtrack, written and performed by Charles DeBray and friends, and also featured one of the early, great pioneers of the sport, Whitney Shields. Whitney was a close friend of mine and I was devastated by his drowning death on the lower Meadow River in 1989. I lost another close friend, Charlie Deaton, on the Blackwater River earlier that same year.

In July of 1986, I conferred with another kayak designer, John Lawson, and he put the seed of using aerodynamic principles in my head. For the next decade or so I would strive to build efficient "wings" in the cross section of the boats. This would improve their performance for Mysteries, Screws, and Cartwheels. This led directly to the design of the Projet which had bumps on the stern deck near the seam area. These bumps produced a bolder, rounder leading edge to the wing, a stronger shape, and would become a characteristic found in all my subsequent squirt designs. The leading edge of the Projet wing still had a bit of a corner, though, and so I tried to round it more by producing the Thunderbird.

The Thunderbird opened a can of worms. People started to exploit the custom sizing ability of New Wave by request-ing chops which were "bumped" up near their feet and down by their knees and yet some other way for the stern. This, in fact, was the beginning of the modern-day science of multifaceted chops. The foot bumps were not specific enough to accommodate all paddlers perfectly. This led to the evolution of the Bigfoot which had foot bumps specifical-ly placed for longer-legged people. The Bigfoot was really designed for Eric Lindberg, to keep him from whining so much about his foot pain. The Bigfoot had too much "air" in front of the feet of mid-sized people and before long I creat-ed the Shred to bring the foot bumps closer to the knee bumps. Around this time I started the first of my many trav-els to Japan, and rodeo was just coming into its own as a cubic and popular "destination sport." It was now gaining in popularity and many of the original experts in the rodeo sport were also squirt boaters.

This is also when my brother Jeff suffered another terrible injury on the New River. He was teaching a squirt clinic and fell over attempting a rocket move in Double Z rapid. He broke his neck on a shallow rock. He remembers being fully conscious and paralyzed, only able to hold his breath as long as possible until he was saved by one of his students at the bottom of the rapid. It was a long and painful recovery, but he did return to full form and went on to found the sport of "Striding," where you run whitewater standing with a ten-foot long paddle. As Jeff was recovering I designed a short squirt boat for smaller paddlers—the Maestro. Soon after this we traveled to Great Britain to teach squirt boating and the Maestro remained as a popular design there for some years.

In the mid-nineties, other designers were experimenting with shapes of their own—notably the Voodoo Rocket by Brian Nicholson, the Angst by Eric Zitzow, the Neptune by Jay Stewart, the Sin and Drain by Aaron Phillips, the Venom by Snakey, the Hissdog and Wishbone by Bill Hildreth, the Surf by Ken Saunders, and a flurry of experimental shapes from Ian Thompson. Many of these incorporated a flatter hull and sharp chines to enable the flatspins on waves which became popular in rodeo boats then. Squirt boating also came to prime time television, with my brother Jeff paddling on an episode of *National Geographic Explorer*, Woody Callaway squirt boating the Grand Canyon with Glenn Frye of the Eagles for the same series, and Jeff and myself paddling in southern Mexico on a first descent of the Santo Domingo River for a series called *Expedition Earth*.

In the late nineties, I came out with a series of flat-spinnable squirt designs also. They were the Fantum, Hellbender, Underdawg, and Fish. They were very short, around eight feet long, to facilitate Cartwheels. Japanese experts like Masaji Okuoka and American C-1 squirt boaters like Barry Kinnen and Chris Manderson were then pioneering "no touch" Cartwheels (in C-1 these are called Irish Whips). The flat hulls of the new designs made this difficult move a bit easier. Unfortunately, Masaji, one of the sport's most promising new stars, died attempting a splat on an undercut rock on the Nagara River in Japan on March 16, 1997. It was another devastating loss for myself and the sport.

The late nineties also saw the popularization of squirt gatherings which were unscored events occurring at popular squirt sites. There were no entry fees, judges, numbers on your chest, clocks, or waiting for the scorers to tell you when you had permission to go for your Mystery Move. It fits the outsider mentality of squirt society, and the vibes are naturally low-key and fun. Another stellar event to begin was the Angst-sponsored Mystery Move contest at Cowbell on the Nolichucky River.

I started doing Loops in the fall of 1996, although spontaneous Loops had happened to many squirtists for years. Loops are basically a barrel roll done underwater. This evolved to Retarded Loops (where the loop occurs as you break the surface of the water), and Light Loops (where you loop mostly in the air from a chest-deep Mystery). In the fall of 1999, I worked through prototypes for the Asylum, a short squirt boat in the mid-inseam size range. It works well for Loops because it has a rounded leading edge. It successfully met the market's demands in the spring of 2000.

An interesting evolution occurred through the nineties when several designers started creating shorter, flatter-hulled squirt boats. One idea was that the shortness might solve the old problem of Mystery Movers tapping their sterns in the last bits of the approach. If the stern wasn't way back there to tap the rock, it would be easier to miss. However, in the late nineties Mystery Movers were still hitting their sterns, even in the short boats. The perimeters for getting into excellent Mysteries is just that tight. And the best downtimes are still being had by the old, long, round, and smooth-edged designs. My theory on this phenomenon was that there are three subtle benefits to the old designs. The fact that they are longer helps them maintain a trace more of the forward speed you need to sustain mysteries. The round-er leading edge means less drag. Sharper corner designs have boundary layer separation which results in drag. This drag registers as a loss of forward speed underwater. This creates stalling and shortens the Mystery. And finally I think the old designs had a higher "tool area" to "float area" ratio. The float area is basically the part of the boat sur-rounding you closely and ending just in front of the feet. The tool area is the section of the ends of the boat with essen-tially neutral buoyancy. This is approximately where, if you cut the end off the boat and duck taped it shut and put it in the water, it would hardly float because the weight to vol-ume ratio (density) approaches neutral buoyancy. This tool area shapes the hydrodynamics of the boat in both the for-ward and wing modes and basically gathers currents to har-vest into downtime. Longer boats have proportionally more tool in front of the feet and way back in the stern. Because the tool is the distant ends of the boat, it has greater lever-age over the mass in the center of the boat than the float area does. This tool to float ratio is proportional because of this. To increase the tool area of a short boat 200 percent

Truly Dedicated Squirtist

might only increase the surface of the entire boat by 15 percent. But it could double the tool to float ratio. To test this theory one would have to create it in extreme where the boat is more than twelve feet long and has wide "current gathering" ends. And this is a possible design future for the sport.

The late nineties found squirt judging in a state of flux with different systems tried at key events. It's possible it will work itself into a flexible and robust system in the next century. The judging will affect what kinds of designs people buy for rodeo and could also create a difference between "cruising" and "competing" squirt boaters. The new breed of gatherers are pretty much into downtime, and some even have especially painful and sinky machines for these events. The lust for downtime drives a lot of paddlers at the core of this sport, but not all of them. You see, it has to do with appetite and tenacity. And if you ever get a really big dose of the big "D" it can dampen your appetite for a while. Some realms are so powerful and violent that the Mystery rider is at the mercy of merciless currents. He becomes a leaf in the wind of a breathless adventure. Your boldness and your vulnerability come face to face at such moments and you are often left humbled. So although there are a fleet of awesome submariners like Jeff Schnelle and the Tall One, there is also a sizable crew who just like their Mysteries "sweeeet!"

In these twenty-plus years, the sport has drifted through popularity and danger but has remained driven by experts who are basically doing what they want to. The science has evolved around the ride and so to be an expert means to have a great ride. Squirt boating, once new and radical, is now retro and eclectic. The sport finds itself diffracted but vibrant, shaped more informally than formally. But the devotees cling to the core, drawn by the lure of being cubically liberated and the unspeakable charm of the mystery.

SQUIRT
FUNDAMENTALS

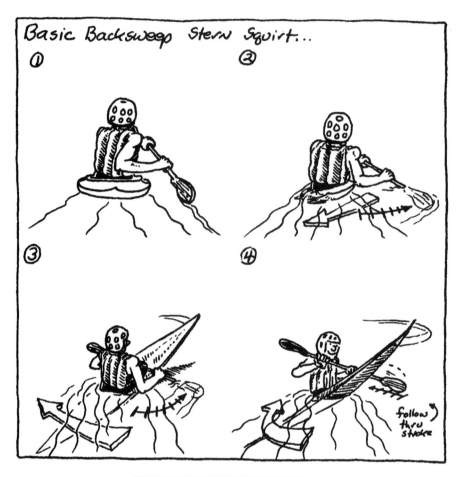

Basic Backsweep Stern Squirt...

① ② ③ ④

follow thru stroke

THE BASIC STERN SQUIRT

Learning to do the basic Stern Squirt properly is not as simple as it sounds or appears. You have to adhere to a lot of details of form; their simple appearance is a charm inherent in all squirt moves. Originated by racers as a quick Pivot Turn, the Stern Squirt has become a popular move involving many tight vertical spins. The best way to learn the fundamentals is through a series of steps on flatwater. Be sure to establish a good solid performance each step of the way.

First, one has to learn the essential move. This can be tough for experienced boaters because they must learn a technique they've already programmed out: leaning to the outside of a turn. Start on flatwater with no current at all. As with any sport, it is essential to learn the feel of the equipment. A lack of current cuts down on the variables in the input you're getting from your new boat. To set up for the key move, put your paddle in position for a backstroke. Take care that the blade is within 18 inches of the stern. Also, tilt the boat with a slight angle down to the outside of the turn you intend to do, opposite the way you would lean a motorcycle. The tilt should be slight, only five to fifteen degrees off of level. Your body must stay centered over the boat, not off to the side; it helps to lean back, too.

As in any move, your stability is a function of how well you stay balanced over your boat. You should never depend on your paddle, as it may break or hit foamy water when you need it most. A fine violinist holds his bow so lightly that it could be plucked from his fingertips at any moment. The concept carries over to kayaking in that if one's paddle hits loose water or a rock, it should not affect the rider because he is centered over his boat. Overly depending on your paddle means you're trying to fudge the move together with arm power in the last moments. It shows lack of charc.

A well-done move depends mostly on the charc, secondly on the timing, and finally on the finishing touches your arms supply. It helps to preconceptualize the move before you attempt it. Here's where "charc in equals charc out" really counts. Visualize a mellow finish to the move and, with this

Hip Bury on a Forward Sweep..
① ② ③ ④

in mind, start a careful beginning. So proceed with the first step as follows: With no forward speed at all, use a long, drawn-out backsweep to sink the hip on the side opposite to the stroke. It is important to sink the hip as smoothly as possible so that it carves underwater. This is the key move. Try this until you can do the move quite smoothly, with your bow rising one or two feet in the air. Feel the timing of it. After the hip is buried, the stern will follow. You punch a hole in the surface of the water with your hip and then fill it with your stern. As in all squirt moves, what happens to the center of the boat determines what will happen to the ends.

The next learning step is to accomplish the "hip bury" with

a single forward stroke. The hip on the stroke side is the one that sinks. Scoop it under. This can't be a long drawn-out stroke, but do try to sink the hip smoothly. The stern will sink slightly also. This is not a squirt move so much as it is training for future moves. It teaches you a brace that's used frequently and acquaints you with the feel of the volume of your stern. This should be done with no forward speed at all and the water has to only skim over the back deck for you to get the feel of the move.

Next, try the backstroke squirt with some forward speed on flatwater. Remember to set up a curved charc. This is a subtle but critical concept central to all squirt moves. This lateral traveling technique helps collect the power of the charc for its transfer into the third dimension. You must set up your form correctly before feeding any power into it. It helps to focus on the path your center of mass will take

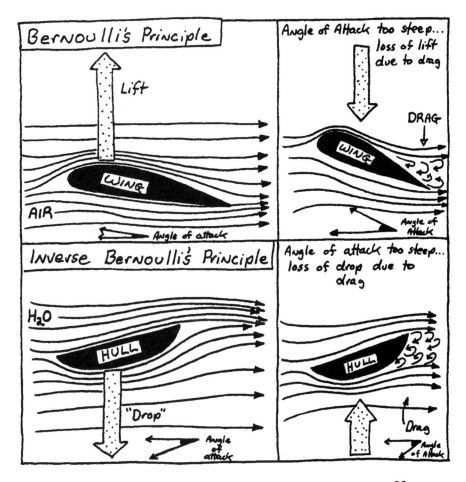

Spinning off a curved charc...

① Set up a curved charc...

② Drift & lean forward to activate rocker...

"spin mode"

③ Begin back sweep & sink hip. Boat nearly perpendicular to current.

④

⑤ Peak move parallel to current

through any particular move. My brother and I use the concept of the "third point." It's not your hull (the first point of contact with the river), or your paddle (your second point of contact), but the "future point" to which you are throwing all your weight. It is anywhere beyond you, in front of your mass in your space-time continuum.

This third point is a very helpful concept. We strive to flow smoothly to our third point though we never attain it. The boat's and river's charcs blend to form the third point's charc. The straighter the third point moves, the more power you can pack into your charcs. Squirt moves involve a transition from stored to kinetic forms of energy and the third-point concept is the discipline involved for maintaining peak energy capabilities. The boat, paddle, and currents will keep you from attaining the third point as they form the move you are doing. The squirtist chases the third point like a mule chasing a carrot dangling from a stick, meanwhile being severely detoured by the boat and water transaction. The third point is always in reference to the center of the boat/rider mass, so concentrate on this area and what is happening there.

Paddle forward at a slow, easy pace. Stop paddling and

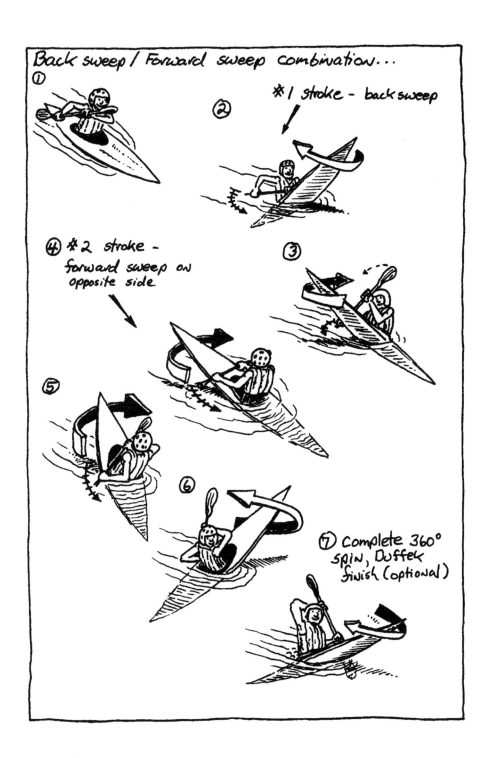

Back sweep / Forward sweep combination...

① ② *1 stroke - back sweep

④ *2 stroke - forward sweep on opposite side ③

⑤ ⑥ ⑦ Complete 360° spin, Duffek finish (optional)

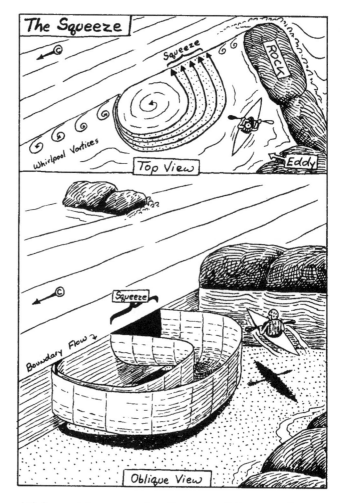

The Squeeze

Squeeze

Rock

Whirlpool Vortices

Top View

Eddy

Squeeze

Boundary Flow

Oblique View

drift forward for a second, setting up a distinct veer. As you paddle forward, lean slightly forward. This sets up a technique I call "activating your rocker." You lean forward on the set-up and then suddenly backward for the squirt. This lets the rocker of the boat help the hull slip into the curvy charcs necessary. When the "held-down" buoyancy of the bow springs up on your cue, it adds energy to the processes sinking your stern.

It is important to use a hip-tilt angle of only five to fifteen degrees. This is because approximately 85 percent of the work done to sink the stern is done by water under the boat, not the water pressing down on the deck. The water flowing under the boat has a longer surface area to cross before it reconnects with the water crossing over the deck. This means it has to travel faster to get to the opposite edge of the boat to reconnect. The faster water speed translates into a lower amount of pressure against the hull, in a freeform version of Bernoulli's Principle. Simplified, this principle states that faster speed directly correlates with lower pressure in a contained fluid. The boat responds to these pressures, moving from the higher pressure on the deck (slower water) towards the lower pressure against the hull (faster water). This describes the basic mechanics of the "drop" principle (opposite of "lift" in aerodynamics), which makes a squirt work. If you use too much hip tilt (angle of attack), the boundary flow starts to separate from the hull. This is the extra-fast flow of water just next to the microeddy generated under the hull. If the cutting edge of your boat were like a rock in a current, the "boundary flow" would be the current side of the eddy line, just next

33

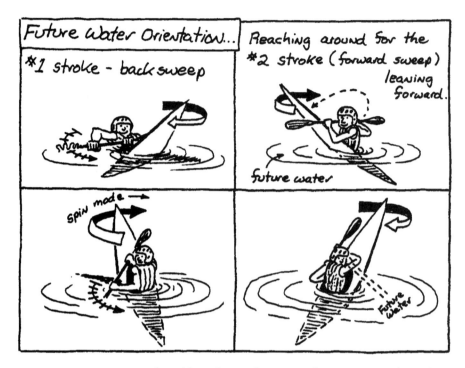

Future Water Orientation...

*1 stroke - back sweep

Reaching around for the
*2 stroke (forward sweep)
leaning
forward.

future water

spin mode →

future water

to the eddy and extending up to where it contacts the rock. The idea is to keep the boundary flow as close to the hull as possible. If it separates, the hull's working surface is reduced, retreating towards the cutting edge. This reduces the amount of work that can be done by the working area (where the boundary flow contacts the cutting edge).

This working area is the key factor in the drop potential of the boat. Letting the water do its maximum potential work allows the rider to save his energies for more noble causes, like maintaining charc power. With the proper hip tilt, the boat also sweeps into the turn faster and then uses this efficiently converted energy to sink the stern. The forward directed mass/energy is converted first to a turning (two-dimensional) mode and, then, using the drop principle, into the third dimension. The energy ends up in a stored form as trapped buoyancy. Letting the trapped buoyancy back up releases the energy back into the second dimension. After the boat reaches its peak possible stored energy, level your hip angle to slow the stern's return to the surface. You are now at what is called your "stern station" and you should be able to free both blades from the water just for an instant. To have the boat level side to side and have your back perpendicular to this sideways leveling means to be "squared up" in your station. Tougher moves require this technique and you can use "cleaning your stations" as a valuable tool for regrouping technique and balance. So learn it early and concentrate on it throughout—when the end of the boat hits its lowest point you need to be squared up over your station, preferably with both blades cleared for an instant.

Important points to remember for this simple flatwater Stern Squirt are: 1) set up a curved charc, 2) activate your rocker, 3) start the backstroke with the blade within 18 inches of the stern, 4) sink your hip and flow to your stern station *smoothly,* and 5) clean your station by being squared up with your blades free for a moment.

Next, try the squirt while facing upstream in a current. Establish a slight ferry charc so you can push sideways into the grain of the current. Your bow should travel from pointing upstream to its peak amplitude as it points downstream.

Back-cut Squirt

If you're really on a roll, try continuous spins with your bow in the air. Use whatever forward and backward strokes are necessary to keep it going but don't make a fool out of yourself—just get used to it. Think about how the third point has to move. Work this technique until you are quite confident and can perform the move aggressively and smoothly. Establish a lateral momentum that folds down into the grain.

Now, it's time to try the squirt going into an eddy. For the first few attempts, use a very broad charc or enter the eddy with a ferry angle. Using a very curvy charc, cross over the eddy line and move well into the eddy. Doing your first few attempts in the heart of the eddy helps simulate the flatwater conditions of the learning stage. After you are more proficient at it, proper form requires doing the squirt on the eddy line, where you can tap back into the downstream currents to revitalize the squirt. A proper squirt bounces from the eddy to the downstream currents and back, with each rebound stoking energy into the squirt.

An important technique to establish is a three-dimensional reading of the eddy. It is necessary to read where the "squeeze" is. This is where the strongest currents of the eddy are pitted most directly against the strongest currents of the downstream sort, and where the peak amplitude of the squirt should occur. Your charc should let the bow climb and turn as it approaches the squeeze in order to tap maximum available energy from the currents. If the squirt starts in the squeeze, it will only proceed into weaker currents. There is tremendous potential energy in the squeeze in a static form. The energies are in a state of dynamic equilibrium. The more active currents in the vicinity are better suited to aid in the active segment of the squirt sequence. The static squeeze is best suited to hold the static portion of the squirt sequence. The move must match the forms found in the currents.

Another essential feature of a perfect squirt is control of the exact direction the bow points at its peak amplitude, the "peak point." The peak point must be orchestrated to tap maximum energy from the currents. If you are doing a squirt going into an eddy, the peak point is behind you as you approach. It is opposite the direction you originally throw your third point. The boat spins 180 degrees to reach the peak point in the squeeze. If you don't hit your peak point in time, don't try to attain any more amplitude. With good form, the peak point will focus on the heart of the squeeze. Think of it as a pole vault. You run to a point, and just before you get there, you turn around to plant your stern. Your bow climbs to peak amplitude with your stern acting as the pole. When the squirt peaks, you should be facing in the direction from which you came. This peaks your form so you can be ready for the next transition into future currents. The cross section of your boat should align thinwise (laterally or

Perfect timing can occur anytime, anywhere.

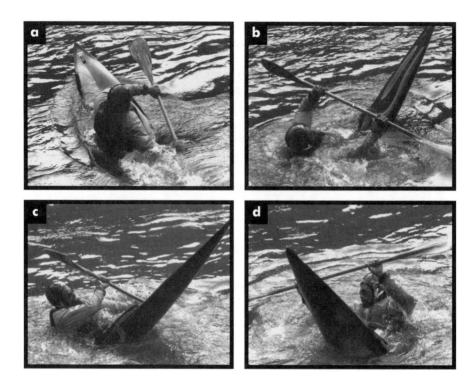

Stern Squirt Sequence

With the blade within a foot of the stern (a), start the number-one back-stroke (b), peaking the squirt with the number-two slap stroke (c), and bringing the bow into a spinning exit with the Duffek (d).

sideways in the water) with the parallel folds of the grain of the current. Think of the cross section as a blade that must cleave into the laminar patterns of the water. Work into and out of the peak point smoothly. A smooth hip bury and rounded charcs help with this facet. You must gather all these details—rounded charc, activated rocker, third-point awareness, backstroke, hip tilt, squeeze position, and peak point—into one scenario of simple perfect timing.

Perfect timing is a real thing. We can't conceive of its implications because they are beyond the constraints of time, and we are not. Nevertheless, we try to achieve it for it is real enough that we can share in it for brief periods, and give our endeavors a sense of cause and direction. It is difficult to attain because we must let it happen without forcing it. Perfect timing is the reward for honing your abilities to their impeccable best. It has much to do with intent, concentration, fluidity, and completeness. Use time as a tool and let each step have its place. Perfect timing is an attitude-altering experience. Simplicity of motion is its only hallmark.

Once the introductory steps have been mastered, you must prepare for future games. This includes both what you want to do and what the river wants to have happen. The first step for preparedness is the number-two stroke of the basic two-stroke combo that makes up what is considered good form. This is a forward stroke on the side opposite the original backstroke. It acts as a brace, guides the proper weight throw, and puts the polishing touches on the amplitude and direction of the bow. Reach around the vertical spinning boat to reach for the "future" water so that the stroke doesn't play out too early. It helps to keep your nose close to the boat. This keeps a minimal cross-sectional profile exposed to the water as you spin, and so reduces the friction that would slow your spin. Reaching for the number-two stroke becomes more important the closer the boat is to vertical. During a Screw Up, a past-vertical move, it is essential to do the reach early and under control. The way you reach controls the nature of your weight throw into the spin mode. Learn to rely on this stroke as a brace, but never let the blade bury underwater.

Concentrate on the angle of your hip tilt as you spin. This is a factor in how your weight is set over the boat. Your weight can be towards the inside of the turn in the beginning for stability. When you are ready for the squirt to turn faster, though, it is necessary to shift your weight towards the outside of the turn. The first step to attaining control over this facet is to try sitting over the boat with no hip tilt; that is, level as it spins. To shift your weight to the outside of the turn, focus more and more emphasis on the number-two stroke. If you can really focus some weight on the stroke, you will find your weight has shifted to the outside of the turn, and so the squirt spins faster. Although it may seem unstable in the beginning, you will find your weight moving to a point where it will find a dynamic stability. This is because you are in pursuit of the third point, which should be moving around and up. A very nice follow-up to this stroke, especially on wry vertical squirts, is a Duffek on the inside of the turn, which guides the descent of the bow.

Now you can try a squirt as you exit an eddy. Charc just above the squeeze so your peak amplitude occurs as you drift into its heart. Start the upstream hip tilt just as your toes cross the eddy line. This is also the cue for when to activate your rocker. Notice that right after you attain the peak point, the boat reenters the eddy. Keep carving your hip into oncoming currents with orchestrated peak points. Any format but this will leave you fighting the currents. A common mistake is to leave the eddy too fast, with too much hip tilt, in an effort to peak out early. Try to establish smooth form before you go for amplitude.

Take care not to hit rocks with your stern. There is a lot of stored energy in the tip of the boat. When it is stopped suddenly by a rock, the effects can be shattering. The evolutionary acceleration on the rock has been estimated to be around five thousand years. The karmic whiplash on yourself can literally tear abdominal muscles and tendons. It also makes your squirt look a little weird and unplanned. In time, you will learn to read how deep an eddy is and tap rocks quite infrequently. You can spot intelligent squirtists because when they hit a rock, they try to avoid it the next time. There are others, though, who keep chipping away, doing irreparable damage to their images. Consider hitting a rock as a crash course in charc correction. Submerged rocks often create boils that actually repel the boat as it approaches. It helps to sink the stern slowly in questionable waters.

A Back-Cut Squirt is where the spins of the squirt move in opposition to the whirlpool energies. It is easy to do but will stall the spin sooner or later. Simply approach the eddy line with a lot of lateral energy and a steep charc. Press your hip under parallel to the grain, causing the bow to arc back into the eddy as it rises. This is the basic charc involved in Rock Splats.

In review, I would say the main area of focus should be on the center of the boat and its progress in pursuit of the third point. All the other techniques should be mastered so that they are done automatically. If you're not smooth, you're doing something quite wrong. The move should look simple and feel like you are falling down into the grain. Try to make ready for a clean exit each time, as this is the sign of a controlled endeavor.

Focus Points
1. Use a curvy charc with lateral momentum.
2. Activate your rocker and effect the hip tilt as your toes cross the eddy line.
3. Start backstroke with your blade near the stern; wait as long as possible.
4. Use a five to fifteen degree hip tilt.
5. Focus your peak points on the heart of the squeeze.
6. Pay attention to the center of the boat and its pursuit of the third point.
7. Control spin speed by reaching for the number-two (forward) stroke.
8. Clean your station and exit under control.
9. Above all, have fun. No one's perfect, but we can all have fun.

THE BASIC BOW SQUIRT

The basic Bow Squirt requires more complex techniques and principles than those used for the Stern Squirt. The "wing" principle, which makes the stern drop for the Stern Squirt, has much less influence here. Instead, the main work is done as a result of the boat pearling in its own wake. Weight throw, and proper stroking and timing, are much more sensitive matters which require more insight. Beginners often find the move awkward because they aren't used to having their bow sink to vertical in flatwater. This new experience can divert your attention from the proper technique, which must be adhered to throughout. It takes time to get used to spending long intervals balanced over your bow. Although beginners often need to apply a lot of effort to attain verticality, experts can do the entire 90-degree conversion without a blade in the water. This is another classic example of a tough squirt technique that appears to be simplicity itself. Again, it is best to start in flatwater.

Since the key ingredient is a successful "pearl," this tech-

nique should be learned slowly and with insight as to the feel of the move. The complexities of a good squirt will confuse an unguided course. To begin with, the squirtist must become quite familiar with the shape and proximity of his wake. By way of introduction to your wake, paddle briskly forward and then drift. After a second, feel how your little (one- to three-inch) wake picks up your stern and gives you a little surf forward. Now, what would happen if you leaned forward during the mini-surf? The bow pearls—a little in the first few attempts, and deeper as we get more aggressive. This is not the key to good technique. Timing is key.

The secret to effortless Bow Squirts, timing, involves two aspects. One of these is creating a well-shaped wake that peaks quickly and predictably. This can be done simply by perturbing the wake to a high crest with just a few accelerating strokes, each one faster than the last. Without perturbing the wake higher, you are only perpetuating it. The idea is to create a peak of power and harvest it on the rebound. The strokes should be crisp and well directed. (If we plant mediocre seeds, what kind of crop should we expect?) This can only occur with a well-intended charc, the most complex issue of the Bow Squirt, which will be discussed later.

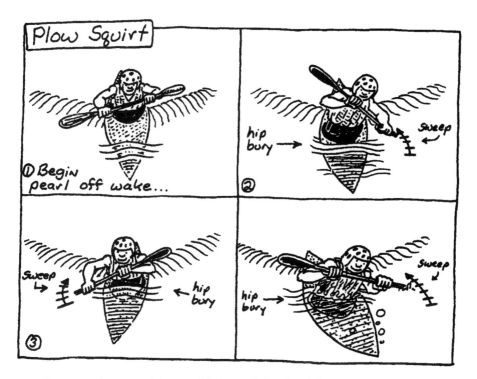

Plow Squirt

① Begin pearl off wake...

② hip bury → sweep

③ sweep hip bury

hip bury → sweep

The second aspect of the pearl is the well-timed weight throw. The idea here is to get maximum boost to the stern at the time when the wake has its maximum energy. This requires insight as to the position of the wake behind you, which can only be attained through feel. Just lean back slightly on your stern as you are drifting forward; when the lift energy starts to affect the boat, activate your rocker by leaning forward suddenly. This rocker activation is the inverse of the one used for the Stern Squirt. Try to accomplish the entire bow bury within a very short distance, or you will run out of wake energy.

Sometimes it is helpful to use what we call a Plow Squirt, preferred in many situations because it is relatively easy on the body and is surefire, especially in turbulent waters. It is a good lead into all Bow Squirts as it can accomplish the first few degrees of drop easily. The Plow Squirt was developed by Jeff Snyder (my brother) as his answer to the more popular Crossdraw technique. He didn't feel like tearing his stomach muscles, a common complaint about the Crossdraw technique. His endorsement and perfection of this technique gave it significant credibility in its early history when people were inclined not to use it because of its forced

Crossdraw Bow Squirt

① Veer off peak of wake, lean forward, plow stroke on side opposite peak...

② As bow pearls, initiate crossdraw/crossbow sweep sequence...

③ Complete crossbow sweep. Use peak of wake to max out your pearl.

④ Follow through.

appearance. By using strong hip tilts he could sink his bow in just two or three strokes. The Plow Squirt involves paddling forward hard after the bow has begun to pearl. These strokes must be powerful, drawn-out sweeps accompanied by a proper hip tilt. The hip tilt must be away from each stroke to help the bow cut, or wedge, under. This is a subtle but essential technique. It can confuse the timing of the pearl, however, because it generates a second wake, which meshes with the first and disguises it. Still, it is advisable to use a Plow Squirt as a prelude to any Bow Squirt as it will establish excellent bow position without sacrificing momentum or control.

Another facet of a well-done Bow Squirt has to do with the kayak's position on its wake. After the wake is well established, the boat should veer to either side of its peak. This sets up a position where the dropstroke will pull the boat back onto the wave's peak as it crests under the boat. The dropstroke is the stroke used to drop the bow and can be a backstroke on the inside of the turn, a forward sweep on the outside of the turn, or a crossdraw on the inside of the turn.

The Crossdraw technique was the original format for Bow Squirts but is possibly the most difficult. This is where the going gets tough. The Crossdraw is not only apt to tear gut muscles, it can fail totally, ending dangerously with the squirtist snagging his blade on the wrong side of the bow and falling over helplessly. Using a slight Plow Squirt here is a handy little secret. If you can use it to cheat and sink the bow about a foot underwater before the crossdraw, you will increase the probability of the blade crossing over the deck. The Crossdraw is effective because it correctly shapes the proper angle of weight throw and leaves your paddle in the best position to initiate the powerful, follow-through sweep. The Crossdraw works basically by pulling the boat back against the veer and/or currents. This lateral energy is combined with a diving angle on the bow to produce drop. If you don't set up a veer or crossdraw too early, you will have only the wake energy to pearl with. Concentrate on drawing your knees underwater.

Forward Sweep Bow Squirt ②

① Wt. Throw

③ A. Forward sweep on opposite side stops spin.... Or. ③ B. Continue sweeping to spin. Spin made

45

It is very important to throw your weight between the bow and the blade while doing the Crossdraw. If the bow is at twelve o'clock and the crossdraw blade is at two o'clock, your weight needs to be thrown at one o'clock precisely. This must be premeditated and incorporated into the charc.

Too much or too little veer will make the weight throw ineffective. If the third point moves on one axis, the last part of the setup features the veer and crossdraw splaying in opposite directions with equal resistance. The weight continues on the same line as the veer and crossdraw reconverge, wedging the bow under.

The diving angle of the bow is the last point to study for a Bow Squirt. In the early stages of the squirt use as much angle as you can comfortably control. As the bow reaches its nadir it is important to level the diving angle so you can sit over the boat and regain control for the follow-through. Remember that whatever diving angle/hip tilt you apply, you must remain perched over the boat in such a way that all your support comes from the boat and not your paddle.

After the bow has attained its original nadir, the "bow station," approximately 45 degrees vertical, you can begin the follow-through. At this point, your forward momentum has completely died, the boat's diving angle has leveled, and your blade has just crossed to the "right" side of the bow and is poised in position for a forward stroke. You are also probably facing 90 degrees to the original third-point charc. The follow-through merely involves a series of quick forward strokes that initiate and maintain the spin mode. The angle of the bow comes into play during the spin if you want to attain more verticality or bring the boat back to surface

Forward sweep bow squirt

Strong current!

Summary...
① ② ③ ④ ⑤ ⑥ ⑦

level. Note that a well-balanced Bow Squirt will leave the
boat at about 50 or 60 degrees, as this is the position
where the rider's weight is most comfortably stationed over
the buoyancy of the bow. Beginners should spend a lot of
time perched over their bows to establish familiarity and stability in this new mode. Always consider your exit, as it is the
final statement of your control or lack thereof.

There are two modes in which you can use currents to
help the Bow Squirt. The first involves using currents to press
the bow down as your strokes drive against them; the second is harder to conceive. It requires finding dead areas in
the current and charcing into them so that you can simulate
the effects of a flatwater squirt. These dead areas are everywhere, and finding them is a real joy. Sometimes they
appear right in front of you unexpectedly. Often, they are
found on downstream or lateral charcs. They are seams, pil-

Bow Squirt Sequence

The cross-bow draw will pass over the deck when it is about one foot under.

lows, or anywhere the currents cancel each other out. These are also the areas where one can accomplish Mystery Moves and Mush Moves. Remember to approach such an area with a charc nearly perpendicular to the axis of the dead area. Try to cheat on your Bow Squirts and use a bit of a Plow Squirt on your approach. Do this subtly and quickly so that people can't see what you did and cop your charc. (That should inspire them to buy this book, which will finance the international trips I have planned for my golden years.)

A classic Bow Squirt, going into or coming out of an eddy, requires a very steep charc. Don't purchase the bow under too strong or too many currents or the river will upset you. Watch out for the future water into which you will be feeding your bow. Keep your blade from getting too involved by using choppy, shallow strokes. The principles of weight throw and wake pearling still apply. Notice how the classic Bow Squirt spins in opposition to whirlpool energies. There is also a version that spins with them. This requires a very sophisticated charc. Concentrate on developing a lateral momentum that bows you into the eddy line as if it were a seam in the currents. This is a super steep charc. You harvest the lateral force by accentuating the rocker activation. This method is the lead into Mystery Moves.

Another way to sink the bow is to use a forward sweep. This drives the boat against prevailing currents and/or the boat's own veer energy and combines with a diving angle on the bow to wedge the bow under. This works well against very strong currents or too much veer but provides minimal drop by the time the sweep has played out. Another "normal-side" stroke one can use to sink the bow is a backsweep on the outside in the case of a veer, or upstream side if you're exiting an eddy. This is a super-safe stroke, as it is really a glorified low brace. A good follow-through for this backsweep method is to stop the rotation of the boat after the initial stroke, and, with the same blade, do a forward stroke that starts the boat spinning the opposite way. Then, use a diving angle on the bow to sink it even deeper. This bow-squirt method is the same as in the Smash, the tough half of a Cartwheel. Both of these methods require advanced "feel" and timing but, in the long run, are safer. However, they are relatively slow and leave the paddle in an ineffective position after the initial drop. They are worth learning because they are the basic techniques used for transitional moves while blasting.

In conclusion, while a good Bow Squirt appears to be effortless and fast, it is the result of a charc set many feet and seconds in advance. Focusing on your knee area is helpful. If you sink this area cleanly and deeply, then the bow will have done so also. Keep your arms close to your body as you are in danger of pulling or tearing muscles. Try to use clean exits. Super-charged bow-squirt moves come from efficiently transferring energy from the first dimension, through the second (spinning) dimension, and into the third (Ender) dimension. The spin is the transfer mode, and more spin provides more of a grace period while maneuvering. Once you've mastered the basic Bow and Stern Squirts, you're ready to move on to the "transitional" moves: Cartwheels, Mystery Moves, and such. Constantly work on cleaning up your basic moves as this is the key to timing in the more complex moves. Remember to preconceptualize the move and adhere to the river's demands for proper timing. Don't fall on your face.

Focus Points
1. Use accelerating strokes to perturb a high wake.
2. Set up a veer charc.
3. Activate your rocker or use a slight Plow Squirt.
4. Drift long enough for your wake to catch you and pearl your bow (10–15 feet).
5. As the bow pearls, use a diving angle and crossdraw to snare the bow under.
6. Throw your weight between the bow and crossdraw blade.
7. Use spin to establish a grace period.
8. Use a clean exit, i.e., descending spins, Bow Screw Up, or Double Ender.

THE DOUBLE ENDER

The Double Ender simply involves flipping the boat vertically end for end, with the bow traveling from underwater-ender style to skyward-backender style. The move is done laterally and is fast, flashy, and easy. I developed it as one half of the Cartwheel "dream" I had early in squirt history. Back when squirt boats were comparatively large, it seemed a natural evolution to let the bow spring quickly out of the water after a Bow Squirt. The fact that the stern sunk was actually a nice surprise and a key clue to the possibility of Cartwheels.

The baby Arc enabled us to refine the move in the spring of 1983, which also saw the early stages of the Smash, Cartwheel, and Screw Up. All these moves were a natural evolution of perfected Bow and Stern Squirts and the desire to combine them. I did the first Cartwheel in January 1983 in flatwater on the Cheat River. It was one of the first squirt moves done by the baby Arc. As the ultimate low-volume boat, the baby Arc was the craft in which many 3-D moves were first conceived and accomplished. It gave me a performance standard for judging future designs, as I was striving for more comfortable ones. Although the boat was designed originally for myself, it is commonly associated with my brother Jeff and his early accomplishments. While polishing his moves in it, he proved not only squirtech's expert status, but also its potential: unfettered imagination. He also used it to prove the "dense-boat theory," which holds that a small boat is more stable in heavy whitewater than the surface boats commonly used. By making many squirt moves look quite easy, Jeff cemented their credibility. The science of letting the boat do the work had its origins here with the modern-day evolution into the study of the power of the charc.

The Double Ender is easy to perform, but it's a critical step towards expertise in the squirt world. It is a sign that the rider

Double Ender

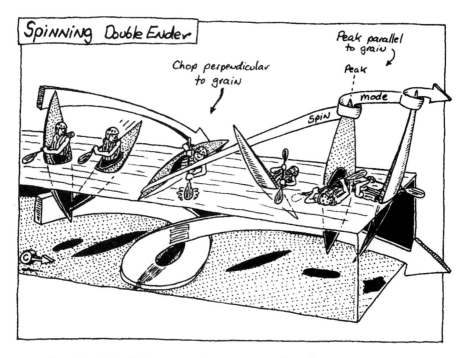

Spinning Double Ender

Chop perpendicular to grain

Peak parallel to grain

Peak

mode

Spin

is comfortable with both the Bow and Stern Squirt and ready to try this easiest of the transition moves. Only with dynamic confidence can this move be honed to the simple maneuver it appears to be. The reason is that the techniques involved are an extension of the control necessary for the basic moves. They require peaking momentum and control to a dangerous new frontier of complex sequences of moves in which the rider is ever more committed and responsive to the currents at hand. It is also the first of several moves that can double as saves in tricky situations and, as such, is indispensable to squirt progress. All transition moves belong to the realm of squirtists who possess super-tuned boats, in which the bow and stern volumes are closely matched. If you don't have such a boat, these moves can do serious damage to both body and mind. Transition moves mark where the sport becomes significantly tougher and more dynamic, opening the door to Cartwheel Splats and Mystery Moves. It is the realm of the unlimited.

Let's start with the easiest transition. First, you need to set yourself in deep water with your bow pointed down and your stern wrapped in sky—your bow station. With practice, you've become quite comfortable with this position and you're ready for a flashy exit. The key concept to understand

Double Ender Sequence

Keeping your weight off to the side of the boat (a), use a simple forward stroke/brace (b, c) to kick the bow skyward (d).

is that the boat must move laterally, that is, sideways, or thinwise, in the water. Other points to keep in mind are maintaining momentum, paddle position, timing, and your position in the currents.

It helps to let the buoyancy of the bow have a maximum effect so it can do the bulk of the work needed. Keep your upper body from encumbering the action of the boat by holding it away from the boat as it flips, almost stationary on the water. In the beginning, you should try this end-for-end flipping at a low (about 45-degree) angle. This takes less effort and provides more stability. Use this technique to establish control over the bow's charc on exit from the move. With just a little practice, you can have the boat spin precisely into the final charc you intend.

Maintaining the momentum of the charc that submerged your bow will feed energy into the releasing of the trapped buoyancy of the bow. Anything that adds spring to this escape helps. The stroke used is a slight forward stroke, done in a plane parallel to the boat's flip.

Notice how when you hold your body off to the side, it actually falls a few inches from the perch it attained through the leverage of the Bow Squirt. When this happens, it helps pop the bow loose and puts some punch into the sinking of the stern in the same moment. Don't worry about having your stern sink deeply, immediately. The move generates perfect momentum and charc for the Stern Squirt, so rely on this fact and be patient. There is a slight pause before you attain your second stern station. Try to feel the timing necessary for the buoyancy transfers. On the initial Bow Squirt, the bow is driven deeply underwater. There will be a slight rebound, or bounce, after the original nadir. Use this bounce to pack extra energy into the flip. If you don't account for the bounce, chances are you will be fighting its effects. All vertical transition moves involve a subtle interplay between the trapped buoyancy of the down end and the center of mass you are parking above it. The mass props itself over the buoyancy over and over with each transition. Focus your form so you do this propping work as smoothly and efficiently as possible.

As in many squirt moves, you can find extra energy and stability by initiating a spin. This lets energy slip from the second dimension to the third and back. It also establishes a lateral momentum, which will help you deal with unexpected strong currents. The spin will help you carve into them, lessening their effect on your stability.

The Double Ender is a beautiful exit to any unintentional Bow Squirts that happen to you during the course of running a rapid. Maintain the momentum of the diving bow and, with a strong forward stroke, flash it back through the sky all the way to your original charc. A final point to study is the angle in which you fold into the grain, during the "chops."

There are three common scenarios for accomplishing the Double Ender: 1) after an Ender, during a surf on a wave, 2) after a Bow Squirt on an eddy line, and 3) after a Bow

Chopping parallel to grain

Squirt in a seam or in a whirlpool. In each case, it helps to pay attention to the angle with which the stern carves into the currents. In most cases, your spinning charc should have your stern start carving in on a broad charc, but spin into alignment with the grain as the verticality peaks and the kinetic energy of the boat plays out. In other words, the knee area can kick out and the hip area punch into the water, nearly perpendicular to the currents. The boat has a lot of power at this point, and can afford to introduce itself to the currents with a bold broad charc. This is appropriate because it assures a better alignment later, when there is less energy available and the squirtist can't afford to fight the currents. If the boat wasn't spinning, this wouldn't be so important. In most cases, especially high-power scenarios, the spin is natural and helpful. The spinning rider needs to focus on having his peak point occur with the optimum alignment already discussed in previous chapters, i.e., parallel to the grain. The broad charc lets the currents kick the boat sideways, just before it attains verticality, and so, feeds extra energy into the spin mode.

One situation where the spin isn't so important is just after an Ender. In this case the boat can do the entire chop parallel to the grain with minimal spin. This is because the move, done this way, will leave the boat with a fine charc, pointing downstream. This format also helps the boat tap into Rocket Move energies, discussed later. These energies play a major role in sustaining Cartwheels in "wave trains." If you're ever in a situation where you lack spin, time the chops so that they are parallel to the grain. This is the path of least resistance, and so allows you to spend your energies re-attaining spin or control.

In the case of seams and whirlpools, the chops are best done parallel to the grain. In a whirlpool, it may appear that the boat is spinning, but it is actually moving parallel to spinning currents. A spin in a seam will move you out of the dead area if you're not careful. Remember, a parallel chop needs to be done quickly, so the alignment is precise for the duration of the inversion. Any time you are put into a Front-Ender mode, you can usually find a decent exit with a Double Ender. The trick is to reach the proper spot in the water with the forward stroke blade, so that it helps but is out of the way. If you are spinning into the Front-Ender mode, reach around the boat, so the working blade contacts the future water and won't play out too early.

54

1. Try to maintain as much ender momentum as possible.
2. Keep your body stable and off to the side of the flipping boat.
3. Set the working blade in future water where it will work but be out of the way. The forward stroke is done parallel to the flipping boat.
4. Let the buoyancy of the bow spring out of the water by timing the "bounces."
5. Set charcs so stations have the wing sections of the boat cleaving the grain of the current.
6. Use spin to maintain control.

THE SMASH

The Smash is the tougher half of the Cartwheel and involves smashing your bow underwater after a Stern Squirt. It was developed around the same time as the Double Ender, as a recovery technique for instances in which the bow comes down hard after a Stern Squirt. Super-low-volume boats, from the baby Arc on, allowed the move to attain true verticality. This is another move that requires a super-tuned, volume-balanced boat. The move demands a radical backstroke/brace that can aggravate shoulder tendons if it's not done smoothly, so remember to let the boat do the work. It is difficult to do the Smash totally vertical, so don't worry about this—just concentrate on coming out of the move smoothly. Currents are a big help and can provide the extra

Basic Smash

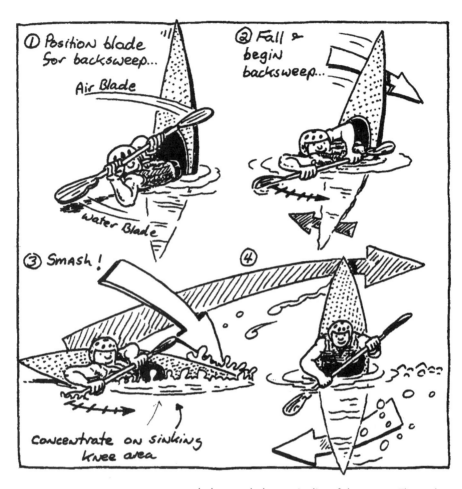

energy needed to peak the verticality of the move. The technique involved here is also the key move needed to make the transition from a Front- to Backblast. It's also a good recovery mode if you ever find yourself backendering involuntarily. When the bow comes down, it continues on the same arc another 180 degrees, all the way underwater and back to the surface, pointing in the same direction as you originally intended.

The Smash is a transition move, and so applies to many scenarios. I will describe a best-case scenario and let the reader extrapolate to any situation where it may apply. Find a clean, tight eddy line with powerful currents. Leave the eddy high and perform a fast Stern Squirt. Try to keep the momentum of the bow, arcing through the sky, over into the charc that brings it back underwater. This is done by means of a powerful, well-placed backstroke. The squirtist must set up the stroke as the boat approaches its stern station. This facet requires that the rider do the initial Stern Squirt with enough control and stability that he can use his "spare time" on the way to the stern station to set up the backstroke. Essentially, the rider must reach very far behind himself, which also happens to be over his head, as the boat is near vertical at this point. It helps to try the first few attempts at a less-than-vertical angle. This provides more reaching room to get the backstroke blade well behind you and the spinning boat.

Compensate for the awkward-reach aspect by 1) doing the backstroke very hard, 2) keeping your face and, therefore, your weight near the water, and 3) letting the buoyancy of the exiting stern have as much effect as possible. Focus on how the super-hard backstroke will make the boat leap backwards as it goes through the transition. This leaves your pushing (low) arm in a position where it can, at one point, do a lot of work. Setting up early lets you wait to do the hardest part of the backstroke when your arm has the best alignment for such work later in the move.

Using this concept will save a lot of wear and tear on your shoulder. The shoulder injury occurs because a major tendon of the rotator cuff, when under stress, will pop out of the groove of bone in which it was meant to work. After popping in and out of this groove several times, it becomes sore and inflamed. This inflammation helps it pop out of the groove easier and easier each time. The problem can become serious enough to take more than a year to heal. That's why you shouldn't try this move unless you have a super-low-volume bow designed for these moves. Remember to do the backstroke with a shallow charc or you will have trouble extracting it from the water after the Smash.

Keeping your face near the water insures that you don't have your weight supported by the boat. It is actually supported by your lifejacket at this position. You will find difficulty moving your "air blade" past the vertical deck to position the "water blade" for the back stroke. Lying back on the water gives you more room for clearance and lets you do the whole move slower. This slowness lets you sense when the buoyancy of the stern wants out. This is your cue to effect the backstroke. Remember to let the boat leap backwards, in response to the backstroke, as this will lessen the resistance applied to your shoulder and help protect it from injury. The move should move sideways through the water about five feet. It's not a one-point end-for-end flip.

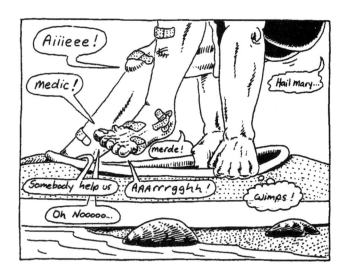

All the points made in the previous chapter, in reference to charc angles compared to grain alignment, apply here also. Essentially, with power and spin, cut in with a broad charc and peak on a steep charc. With no spin, such as seams and wave trains, use parallel alignments to reduce resistance from the grain.

The main area I focus on when I smash is the knee area. If you can force your knees under, the bow will follow. The main work that needs to be done is the sinking of this fat center area, and the propping of your weight above it. By paying attention to the main work area, you won't be under a delusion as to how much work must be done. It will also help you fine-tune the angle of the cross section of the boat, and so, help it effectively encounter the future water. I also think about saving my backstroke until the last possible moment, when the blade is in good position and I feel the buoyancy of the stern trying to surface. To do the stroke too early would prevent the buoyancy from doing all the work it can contribute. Waiting also keeps the stroke from playing out too early, which would reduce its bracing effects later in the move.

In order, I concentrate on 1) charc/timing, 2) clearing my air blade past the deck to position it early for the back-stroke, and 3) waiting as long as possible to do the back-stroke. Remember that spinning adds grace and magic to any move, so go for it. A good rule of thumb to remember is "spin equals flash." It also keeps fellow boaters from crowding your space.

Focus Points

1. Set up proper charcs per grain/spin encounter.
2. Let the bow travel *through* its peak point without pausing.
3. Clear the air blade across the deck to set up back-stroke early.
4. Save the backstroke until the last possible moment.
5. Keep your face near the water and let the boat leap out backwards.
6. Let the stern's buoyancy do as much work as possible.
7. Concentrate on sinking the knee area.
8. This is an excellent recovery for a past-vertical squirt.

CARTWHEELS

As the name implies, Cartwheels are an end-for-end flipping of a boat. The move is accomplished laterally, or thinwise for your wing sections, and can be done anywhere it is deep enough. The dream of easy Cartwheels has been a guiding force through the evolution of squirt designs. And, in fact, this simple transition move (trading end for end) is what led to Mystery Moves. While the concept is simple, the deed is not necessarily easy.

A continuous succession of Double Enders, followed by Smashes, is the crux of the move. The timing of each flip is dictated by the boat's alignment with the current and by the squirtist's stability and position. If you are just learning the move and are working in flatwater, don't worry about doing truly vertical flips. A lesser angle will suffice to teach the proper strokes and weight throws. The "maintained momentum" concept must be carried through to the charc of the third point occurring near the center of the boat. The motion of the third point is closely tied to the buoyancy of this center area and the way you prop your weight over it.

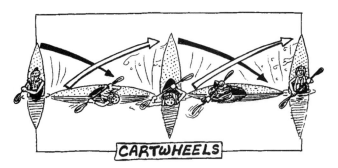

CARTWHEELS

60

The main area of focus should be on burying the knee and pushing the boat backwards with the backstroke.

An expert Cartwheeler times the boat's flips with the bouncing of the center area's volume. After a flip, the boat sinks a bit, in response to the way the rider fell off the previous buoyancy. The next flip is timed to harvest energy from the rebound of the buoyancy. If, when peaked, a Smash has driven the bow very deep, then, as it bounces back up a bit, the squirtist works the lateral flip of the Double Ender—the bounce energy transfers to the laterally charcing bow on its way back to the air. The boat will do most of the work for you, if you follow this formula for timing.

The alignment of the boat, as it cuts into the currents with each flip, can help or hinder the move also. The idea here is the same as described for the Smash and Double Ender: the boat can chop through the surface nearly perpendicular to the current, but the spin of the boat should have the wing sections cleave the grain of the current as the boat approaches its stations. The Cartwheels are performed as a series of stations with the Smash and Double Ender getting you from one to another. Again, the trick to cleaning your stations is to have the boat level side to side and have your back squared up to it with your blades free for a moment. If the current/charc alignment is not correct, the system will dissipate energy from the move, and it will come to an end. A graceful ending requires realizing when the energies are waning and performing a decisive conclusion to the series. This usually means descending spins on a Stern Squirt, pointing, finally, to the precise point you desire. Although it is not a mistake to do your chops completely parallel to the grain throughout, you will find this alignment doesn't add any energy to the move. It is nearly impossible to work par-

Cartwheel Sequence

A cartwheel is a Smash (a, b, c) followed by a Double Ender (d).

allel to the grain in a no-spin mode. You also lose your pivot point near the center of the boat, because too much alignment will "marry" the boat to that piece of current; you will proceed downstream with it, unable to mesh into other currents. This negates the leverage normally involved as you transfer from the second to the third dimension. It reduces the rebound effects that add spin to moves.

Remember to maintain momentum in the ends of the boat. Use brisk, dabbing strokes, as this will keep your blades from becoming too involved with the water. The deeper and more involved the stroke, the harder it is to extract, and the slower your reaction time will be.

Focus Points

1. Use strict discipline on peak points, buoyancy bouncing, and grain alignment.
2. Work at less-than-vertical angles if necessary.
3. Finish the move under control by deciding early enough.
4. To supercharge the move, work at past vertical angles.
5. Use spin to reestablish control; reach for future water while spinning.

6. In wave trains each peak point should correlate to the wave crests.

"CLEAN" MANEUVERS

A "clean" maneuver is one done without a stroke. The paddle blades, if any, stay in the air throughout. The first clean Cartwheels I saw were done by Barry Kinnen and Chris Manderson as "Irish Whips" in C-1, sometimes during their raging "Mobiusequences" where they hit all points on a three-dimensional compass many times over. Then Masaji Okuoka perfected the moves in a kayak, which is considerably more difficult because you sit lower in the boat and have less weight to throw. He was perfecting his clean stalls just before he died. This is where you throw a few cartwheel ends without a stroke and then freeze on end and reverse the Cartwheels. You can also do clean squirts, where you initiate a Stern Squirt and ride it out without a stroke, and clean screws where you break out of the eddyline with a single setup stroke and then bust all the way through a Stern Screw without a stroke. Most clean maneuvers require a lot of concentration and so they are often best done in calmer waters, although this is not necessary.

Besides focusing on currents, clean maneuvers require special techniques. Most people start with their bow down because it is an easier and calmer way to get started. Start with low Cartwheels, maybe with the ends getting just a foot

Clean Cartwheel Finesse

Detail: wing's angle of attack between stations

Backbone stays upright while abs and hips set wing angle

Left stern edge feathered at slight angle of attack

"Clean" Stern Station

"Square"

← denotes "attacking wing"

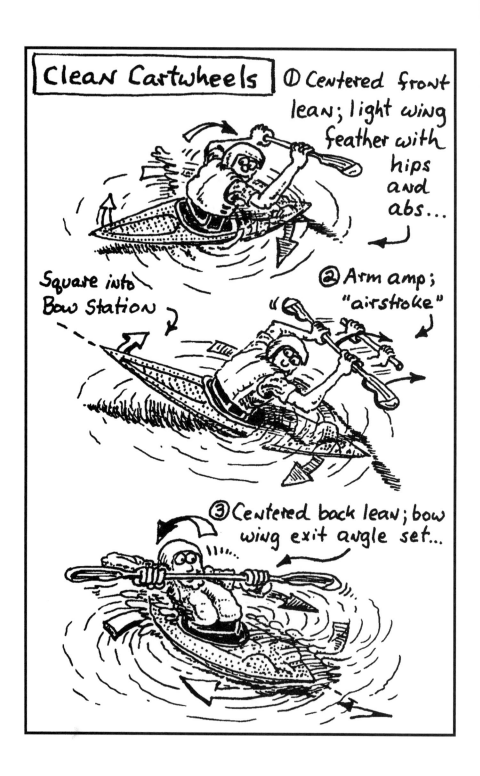

Clean Cartwheels

① Centered front lean; light wing feather with hips and abs...

② Arm amp; "airstroke"

Square into Bow Station

③ Centered back lean; bow wing exit angle set...

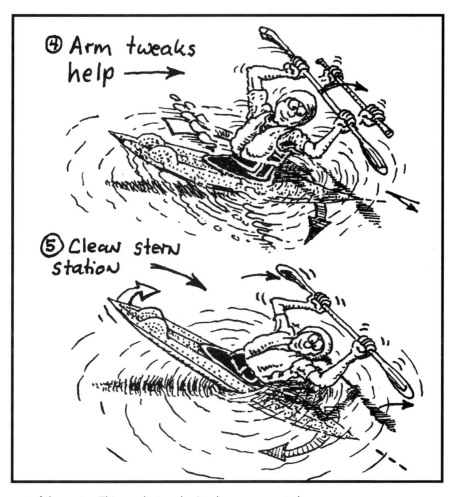

④ Arm tweaks
help ——→

⑤ Clean stern
station

out of the water. This modest realm is where you must do
your learning, so try to make sure no one is watching. There
are a number of things to concentrate on all at once, but
the key technique for success comes from being sure you
are throwing your weight over the ends of your boat and
not off to the side. All the cartwheeling and lateral motion
comes from feathering the leading edge of your boat with
your abs and hips. You throw your weight over the end of
the boat with your hips and abs holding a slight angle of
attack for your wing edge. This is where most people lose it.
They fall too hard, off to the side, and with too much angle
of attack. It helps to keep your abs firmed up throughout the
move. And be sure to be squared up just for an instant over
your ends when you are in each station. You must also learn
to get a feel for a slight lateral turning motion the boat will

Clean Cartwheel Sequence

Keep your abs firm to level the boat in each station (a), and keep your body upright as you feather your hip angle to leave your station (b).

develop during Cartwheels. The boat will actually travel as you cartwheel. You simply get a feel for it and go with it. You can also use your paddle for "airstrokes" where you almost touch the water with a stroke but never do. This wee bit of light-touch weight throwing is often just the thing you need to tweak the cruder aspects of the main weight throw. You are actually throwing your weight with your hands and paddle. Use the same motions you would use if you were actually stroking the water for this, but just keep the blades in the air throughout. A technique I have seen the Japanese use to good effect while learning is to just lightly tap the water with a touch brace when need be. You just maintain the flow of momentum and don't let slight touches end your series or affect your concentration.

Perhaps the ultimate form of clean Cartwheels are "Heliwheels." Heliwheels involve performing a full 360-degree paddle spin at each station of a clean Cartwheel. The move looks like a teetering helicopter, hence the name. It was first developed in Japan in October of 2000. Rolly Imaizumi came up with the idea and was toying with it when he introduced the concept to Iwase Hideoshi. Iwase is a clean Cartwheel expert in his Sin kayak and he soon put together Washouts with the full paddle spin. Within minutes he was performing many clean Cartwheel ends with the full paddle spin on each end. He made it look easy. Soon Motoko Ishida was repeating the move and a lot of others were trying too, with mixed results. It's a flashy and fun maneuver which is essentially a demonstration of your control over your Cartwheel charc. Start to learn it with a Washout as Iwase did. Remember the bulk of the paddle spin should occur as you are secure over your station. You don't exactly pause for the spin over your station but you use the stability of the station to get the move accomplished freehanded. You start the paddle spin as you approach the

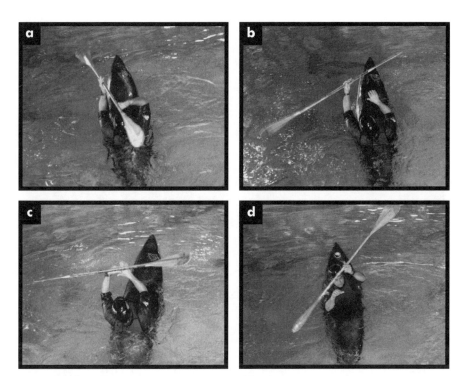

station, perform the crux in your station, and let the spin play out as you leave your station. Then learn to make the transition to your stern station and pull off the next full spin with similar timing. As always, cleaning your stations is key. Let the paddle spins be an enhancement, not a distraction.

Focus Points

1. Start bow down and work low angles.
2. Throw your weight directly over the end of the boat, not off to the side.
3. Use abs to feather the wing ends of your boat into a modest angle of attack.
4. Use your paddle to throw that last little bit of weight.

Heliwheel Sequence

Make sure you are level with your station (a) before you try the twirl. Work with your hands just off-center on the paddle (b). Clean Cartwheel techniques keep the boat moving while your hand work is quick and sure (c). The bow station twirl is easy if you stay centered (d).

SWITCHBLADE TRICKS

I started doing Switchblade Squirts in the summer of 1998. They are a simple and subtle move that evolved to Switchwheels in Japan in the fall of 1999 and Blasting Switchwheels that I started doing at Cueball rapid on the Cheat River in the spring of 2000. The concept behind them is relatively easy, although the execution can be problematic. To do a Switchblade Squirt, you take a forward sweep to ini-

Switchblade Squirt

Blasting Switchwheel

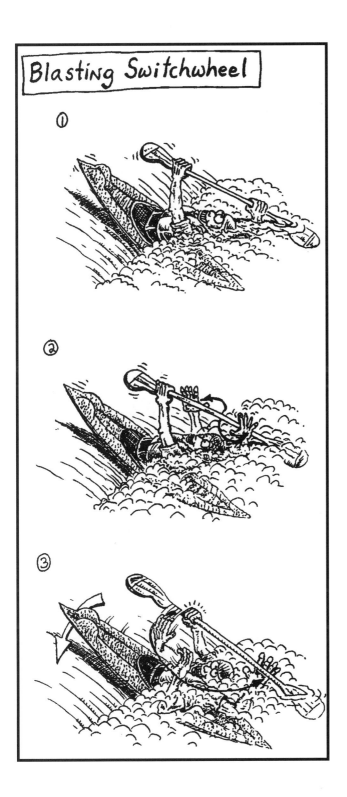

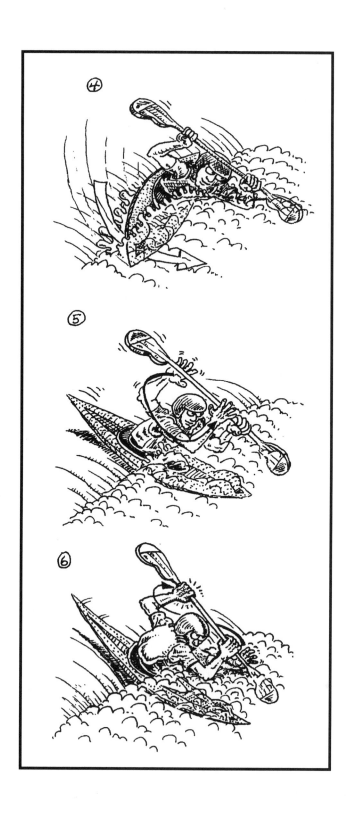

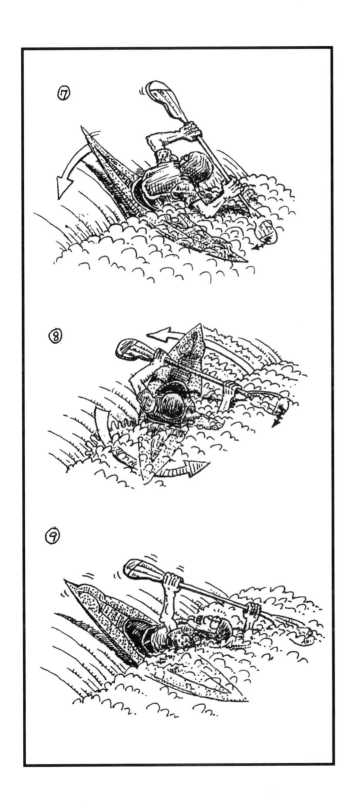

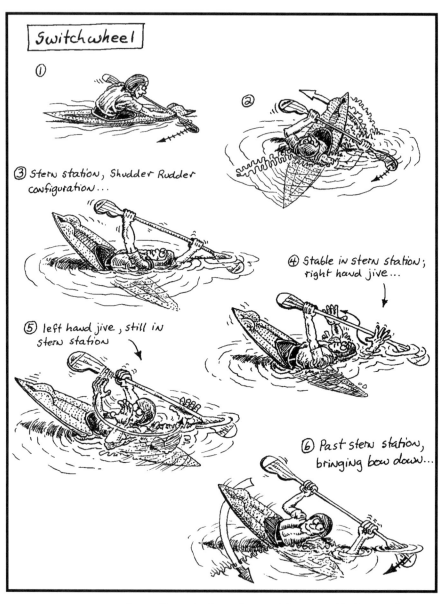

Switchwheel

①

②

③ Stern station, Shudder Rudder configuration...

④ Stable in stern station; right hand jive...

⑤ left hand jive, still in stern station

⑥ Past stern station, bringing bow down...

tiate a Stern Squirt and extend the water blade to well behind the boat as the boat approaches its stern station. At this point the boat is level and stable for a microsecond and you release your grip on your paddle to switch your hand positions. The blade stays immersed in the same spot in the water, but now you are beginning a backstroke on the inside of the turn, instead of finishing a forward stroke on the outside of the turn. The best way to switch your hand positions

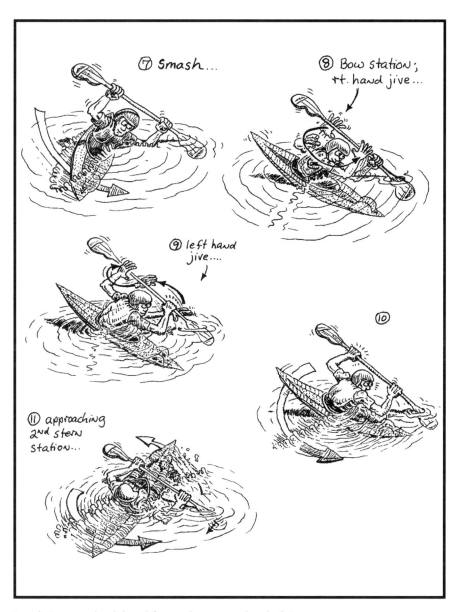

⑦ Smash...

⑧ Bow station; rt. hand jive...

⑨ left hand jive....

⑩

⑪ approaching 2nd stern station...

is to bring your back hand forward to grasp the shaft just behind the front hand and move the "old" front hand to a back hand position. You can think of this as the "hand jive" sequence.

The key to this move is in the timing and positioning for the switch. You want the paddle to be in a static and unpressured situation when you release your hands. The way to ensure this is to concentrate on squaring up over your sta-

Switchblades and Switchwheels

Use a forward sweep on the outside to attain a level stern station in Shudder Rudder position (a). With the boat level, the "hand jive" begins with the release of a single hand (b). The second hand reaches for its new position (c). With the second hand in its new position, you are ready to finish the Switchblade with a Duffek or go into a Switchwheel with a Smash stroke (d). At the other end of a Switchwheel, the stability of a level bow station allows some freedom for the hand jive (e).

tion, even though you are basically laid back in a "shudder rudder" position (see the "Flash Strokes" chapter). This is very important. If you can't level the boat into its station, the move will go awry. Plan on this crux move from the beginning and be very disciplined about maintaining good form through your stations. You can end a Switchblade Squirt with the inside blade becoming a Duffek and controlling the descent of the bow or by having the blade work for a backstroke into a Smash, and thereby setting up a Switchwheel. Switchblades work well on flatwater, seams, or eddy lines.

A Switchwheel is accomplished by doing the hand switch

in both the stern and bow stations. This is much easier to do in flatwater than in the currents. You simply do a Switchblade Squirt and use the switched blade for a deep Smash stroke. When the bow station is attained, make sure you are squared up, do the hand jive, and pull the big Double Ender stroke all the way back into the Switchwheel Squirt mode. There you switch your hands and repeat the process. As in most squirt maneuvers it's helpful to work in modest amplitudes initially. Once you get the knack of leveling into your stations while leaning oddly, the process will come quite easily and you'll quickly find it easy to crank up the action.

Blasting Switchwheels basically use the Switchwheel technique to achieve blasting transitions. Start from a Backblast and use a single forward stroke to transition into a Shudder Rudder, level the boat as you are laid back, and deftly hand jive to set up the backstroke transition into backblasting. It helps to do the switch quickly because a paddle left unattended for long in a foampile tends to wander. The backblasting switch is also difficult and tenuous and needs to be done smoothly and quickly. Once this crux aspect is taken care of though, it's easy to see how this next transitional stroke leads to a Shudder Rudder, where you can reinitiate the process.

These are definitely superfluous, extraneous, and unnecessary maneuvers and should only be attempted in moments of extreme hot-doggery. They're not recommended as standard river running technique. They're more in the league of quasi-lethal "Hey, Watch This!" maneuvers, actually. Still, they can be done without a lot of fuss or muss after you master the techniques.

Focus Points
1. Level the boat into each station.
2. Switch your hands quickly in the moment all pressures are off the paddle.
3. Start slow and low, but don't be afraid to crank it up after you get the hang of it.

BLASTING

Blasting is one of the most fantastic rides squirt boats provide. It is, essentially, a means for surfing holes straight on. This applies not only to slide-type holes but, in advanced cases, pourovers. The name came from a maneuver that I

BLASTING

developed before the squirt era. The ancient move was a
charge from the foam of a slide-type hole upstream, until
your energy plays out on the greenwater ramp feeding into
the hole. It was a crude but fun demonstration of energy.
The present mode is a far more sophisticated form of surfing. It involves a nearly static, dynamic balance of energies
that looks and feels awesome. Jesse Whittemore was the
first truly proficient blaster, that I knew of, in the current
mode. He may have been introduced to the concept by Jon
Lugbill, who, at that point, was the country's state-of-the-art
squirtist. Around the time Jesse was perfecting his blast, he
was becoming the best; my brother and I and others were
just starting to achieve expertise at this maneuver. Jeff quickly became one of the best blasters anywhere in the baby
Arc, but it would be more than a year before he and I would
develop the inverse move, **backblasting**. Blasting is safe,
easy to learn, and fun beyond description.

After you have attained blasting position, you play it by
ear, similar to surfing. Blasting skills, therefore, revolve
around gaining access to the blast. To learn to blast, one
must find a kind hole. This would be a slide-type hole, with
a static area in the foam that is clear of submerged rocks.
The smaller the hole, the easier the learning will be. In the
beginning, the move seems so bold that it takes a lot of
nerve to attempt it. After a little practice, it becomes obvious
that it is the very best way for a squirt boat to ride a hole,
and the squirtist will rarely use any other mode.

There are two basic approaches to a blast. The best way
for beginners starts with the rider sitting sideways in a hole,
riding like in a normal kayak. Maneuver your kayak to one
side of the hole, so that your body is just to the side of the
sweet spot in the very deadest area of the foam. The stern
should be towards this sweet spot and the bow towards the
corner of the hole. The trick, then, is to sink the stern under

the foam so that the boat lines up parallel to the grain, centered in the sweet spot. A strong forward sweep from the foam-side paddle will initiate the move. Next, the rider must do a strong backsweep on the upstream side of the boat. Use the same basic stroke and hip tilt used for the Stern Squirt. A very steep hip tilt is acceptable here because it helps the bow climb over the greenwater rushing into the hole. After the steep charc is attained, basic surfing skills apply. If you are having a hard time at this stage, try a smaller hole or try riding the shoulder of the hole.

Blasting can have a static or dynamic nature. The static blasts are found on the shoulders of the hole and in the exact center of the sweet spot. The dynamic ride requires quick crosses from shoulder to shoulder, dashing back and forth across the sweet spot but never quite homing in there. This type ride applies to holes that are hard to ride because of some underwater feature that perturbs the greenwater below the foam and destroys their normal cradling effects. Squirt boats are so small that they are essentially unaffected by foam structures and surf only on the bowl-shaped understructures of greenwater found with any wave or hole. Any appropriate series of forward or backstrokes will do to maintain the blast. Remember to exit cleanly off the shoulder.

A more advanced approach to the blast is the preferred mode for most dynamic scenarios. This involves lining up with the grain while sitting high on the foam before entering the crotch of the hole. As the foam draws the boat into the crotch, the rider should set a slight angle to establish the lateral momentum technique used with any Stern Squirt. The

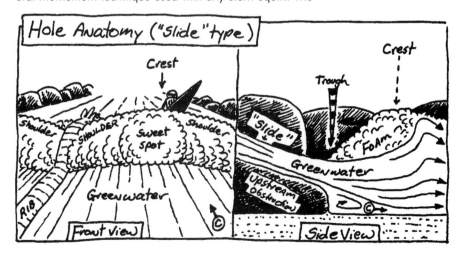

key technique here is to "tilt the boat," so it can drop down through the foam and contact the greenwater early. This sinking must be done before the boat reaches the crotch. This not only stabilizes the boat by reducing the foam's effects, but helps raise the bow up over the greenwater. The hip tilt, angled charc, and leaning-back position all combine to keep the bow from pearling.

Try to find the most static blast possible in the sweet spot. This is often easier said than done, but it helps you feel out the understructure of the hole. If the blaster charges into the blast, the boat will travel very far up the greenwater, upstream of the hole. The currents will then cause a rebound back downstream where the stern will sink very deeply under the foam. The foam will cause a rebound up the greenwater ramp, and so forth and so on. This makes it hard to stable out in the sweet spot. The recommended procedure is to 1) approach with a slight angle to create lateral momentum, 2) use a hip tilt to drop through the foam, and 3) use minimum strokes to keep from perturbing or disturbing the situation.

Blasting a pourover appears to be a truly radical scenario. However, vertical blasting is usually a super stable and controlled ride. The lateral movement necessary to exit the hole is achieved by a vertical version of a ferry angle. Take care not to lose your patience on exiting and set up too broad a charc. This can quickly develop into an out-of-control veer, which will plunge the rider sideways underwater to the understructure of the hole. It's hard to reestablish control of your charc under these conditions. A transition to a Backblast is a workable solution to this situation.

The approach to a Pourover Blast is difficult. It requires all the technique learned in slide-type blasting and more. You generally want to approach on a very broad charc. In the last moments before impact, effect a bow lift with a strong foam-side forward sweep, followed quickly by a reverse sweep on the falls side. The transition to the third dimension must be quick and sure. It helps to have strong lateral momentum directed to a sure exit charc, in case plans don't work out. Some things you may not expect in the vertical mode are 1) the foam will seem to surround you, even up to your ears, 2) your bow could very well extend up over the rock creating the drop, causing a peculiar scene from upstream, and 3) lateral progress, as in exiting, will happen very slowly. It is not unusual to connect with the rock of the

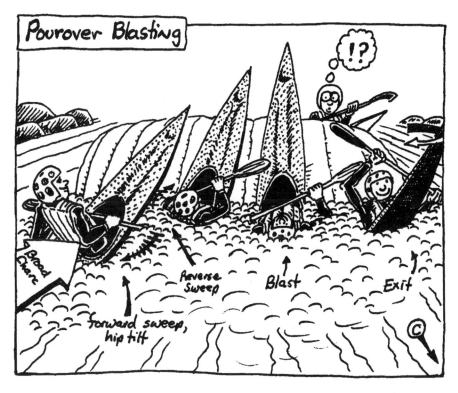

Pourover Blasting

Blasting in the sweet spot can be nearly effortless.

falls. If this happens, work slowly and don't worry as long as there is a good connection with the air. It behooves the blaster to make an accurate read of the depth of the hole, to prevent touching bottom on your way to vertical. Try sticking your paddle down if you can't tell by looking. If you're not sure, don't try the move, as failure in this arena is quite embarrassing. A final note on vertical blasts is that, as far as I know, the exits are usually sure and easy. It is easy to speculate a swirl-o-gram, though, if the blaster spins out too tight in the corner.

Focus Points
1. Establish lateral momentum.
2. Use a hip tilt and backsweep as in stern squirting.
3. Pay attention to upstream/downstream orientation to minimize rebounding.
4. Find the sweet spot to feel out the understructure.
5. Exit under control.
6. Have a blast—it feels even better than it looks.

BACKBLASTING

Backblasting was developed about one year after blasting was first established as a squirt technique. Though it seems to be a predictable evolution, it was inhibited by the large bows (with ample foot room) popular in that era. The move is simply blasting with the bow sunk under the foam instead of the stern as in common blasting. Again, after the original position is established, the rider is on his own and must play it by ear as the river dictates. The proper technique is needed to establish the backblasting position under control. I believe I was the first proficient Backblaster, using the Ride kayak. There are several approaches to a backblasting charc. After a squirtist has become proficient at backblasting, transitions from one mode of blasting to another become easy. Backblasting is one of the most insight-demanding squirt moves. The squirtist can almost close his eyes while studying the feel of his hull brushing the green-water below.

The easiest approach to a Backblast starts with the rider sitting sideways in a slide-type hole. In a manner inverse to the normal Blast, the squirtist must maneuver the boat so the bow is poised, ready to dive under the foam of the sweet spot, and his body slightly off to the side of the heart of the foam pile. While leaning down hard on the bow, you need to put extra emphasis on a hard backsweep on the foam side of the boat. This should snare the bow under the foam pile and, of course, start the stern traveling over the green-water, upstream of the hole. The second stroke is on the upstream side of the boat and tunes the boat into a parallel alignment with the grain. From this point, the blaster should use forward and backstrokes to maintain as parallel a charc as possible. These should be light dabbing strokes, so your blades are not so involved as to slow reaction times. The exit

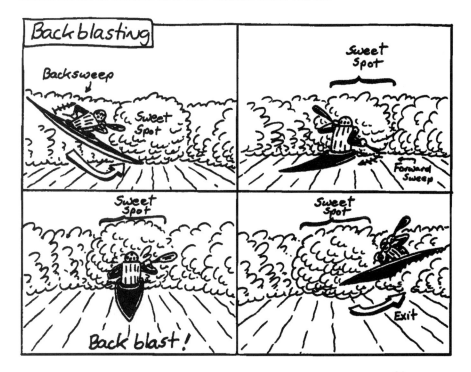

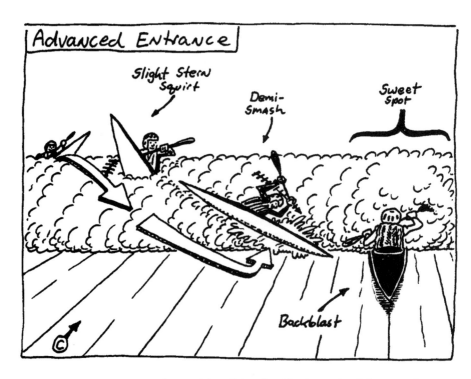

Advanced Entrance

Slight Stern Squirt

Demi-Smash

Sweet Spot

Backblast

can be straight off the shoulder into a back ferry mode or you can do a transition to a forward blast.

Transitions from front- to backblasting are a little tricky but certainly flashy. The main focus should be on the weight throw. Your weight should be thrown across the crotch of the hole, perpendicular to the grain. This will move your weight towards where the boat will travel. If you didn't throw your weight to this point, the boat would tend to move out from under you, which can be quite upsetting. So, from a front blast, you throw your weight to the side as the bow swings around. Your weight will focus to force the bow down under the foam pile. You do all this with a backsweep on the inside of the turn.

Get ready for action, as you will charc into the Backblast with a lot of momentum. Be careful to keep the bow low with a hard lean as the bow swings under the foam, or else your stern can be obstructed by the greenwater shoulder of the hole. If this happens, you'll sink sideways, into the foam pile, and flip into the swirl-o-gram mode. Think of it as going from a front blast to a sideways sit to a Backblast. Do each transition under control, slowly at first. Learn to feel the timing of your charcs, as per their position in relation to the foam pile. If you surge too far upstream, or into the foam pile, or left or right, wait just a second for things to tame down. You could get one or two super-charged transitions but would eventually charc out of control. It's better to proceed methodically and cleanly to let the third point gain its power in a slow-building succession. Remember to execute a clean exit as this will be testament to the control of the ride.

Another way to begin backblasting is on an approach from upstream. With the bow pointing downstream, going at the speed of the current, enter the heart of the foam pile, simultaneously effecting a hard backsweep. On entrance, your charc should be slightly offset, so that the backsweep realigns the boat parallel to the grain. Remember to lean down hard on the bow, as in all modes of backblasting. You should do this by consciously holding your chin as close to your knee as possible. Use peripheral vision to monitor your position, in relation to the heart and shoulders of the hole. Keep your blades out of the foam as much as possible and let the foam press the boat as far upstream as possible. If you enter a Backender mode unintentionally, a strong sideways tilt to the downstream-most side will usually mend your charc. Always be conscious of what lies downstream of the area in which you play. If you exit tired and on a ragged charc, you don't want to find trouble. A controlled exit should be your first priority.

A flashier entrance was developed by my brother Jeff.

Backblasting a Pourover

Broad charc — Backsweep — forward sweep — backblast!

Both this and the previous entrance are very versatile and even apply to starting Bow Squirts in seams in the current. This particular approach involves coming on to the hole on a ferry charc or a **broad** arcing charc. With the bow pointing upstream and swooping in at a good clip, the rider effects a strong backsweep on the hole side, which flashes the bow under the foam, completing a 180-degree turn. Do the move fast and lean down hard on the bow. To sophisticate the approach even more, use a slight Stern Squirt before the Smash-type move. This is a high-control entrance, after you get used to the deeper-than-normal plunge into the foam. A fun follow-up to this move is to backpaddle upstream. The foam will rebound you very far up the greenwater, where you will finally perch motionless for a moment, at least a yard upstream of the crotch of the hole. This is a good time, in the momentary pause, to look at the camera and smile. It helps to have a follow-up to this follow-up, in case the cameraman is a little slow. The boat should return gently to a backblasting mode in the crotch.

Backblasting steep pourover-type holes is quite challenging and exciting. The stern will often protrude over the rock making the hole. Sometimes the rider will find himself chin-deep in the soft foam. Another feature of a steep Backblast is the way the boat will be pressed quite tightly against the falls of the hole. Enter from downstream and execute a hard backsweep to snare the bow under. Follow this with a forward stroke to bring the boat to vertical, before you impact the falls. Again, a controlled exit is the only sane way to go. Do your lateral traveling slowly across the hole, to make sure you don t veer into too broad a charc and fall sideways deep into the foam pile. Remember that you have a limited view of what's coming down from upstream: plan accordingly. If there's heavy river traffic, backblasting will increase your probability of encountering an undercut boat. Safe, sure exits are usually quite easy from Backblasts. With practice, you will learn to control your position in relation to the crotch of the hole/hip alignment and heart/shoulder of the hole alignment.

One final virtue of backblasting that should not be over-looked is the way the technique can be used for sure exits from vertical holes that are not as hospitable as you would like. An errant squirt boat has often cleanly exited a steam-ing, thundering pourover or slide-type hole. Some squirtists have reportedly even been seen scouting what lay down-stream from a backblast. Kids these days.

Focus Points

1. Use an approach charc that will stop the boat near the heart of the foam.
2. Use a hard backsweep and bow lean to sink the bow.
3. Follow up with a soft forward stroke on the opposite side.
4. If the boat tries to backender, tilt it toward down-stream.
5. Be sure to clear the shoulders of the hole during transitions.
6. Use dabbing strokes and peripheral vision to monitor your position.
7. This might be a good opportunity to wash your face.

SCREW UPS

Flashy and complex in appearance, the move is actually simple in nature. One feature that makes this modified Backender different from other squirt moves is the amount of commitment required. It represents the peaking of all available energies with the peaking of control over the ride. Essentially, the squirtist does a fast, high Stern Squirt into a Backender Pirouette, often without even getting his face wet. It's also a recovery move for whirlpool riders—you never flip or get disoriented.

The move began with a dream I had (literally), in which I experienced the first Backender Pirouette squirt of my life. The next day I could remember only one facet of the move

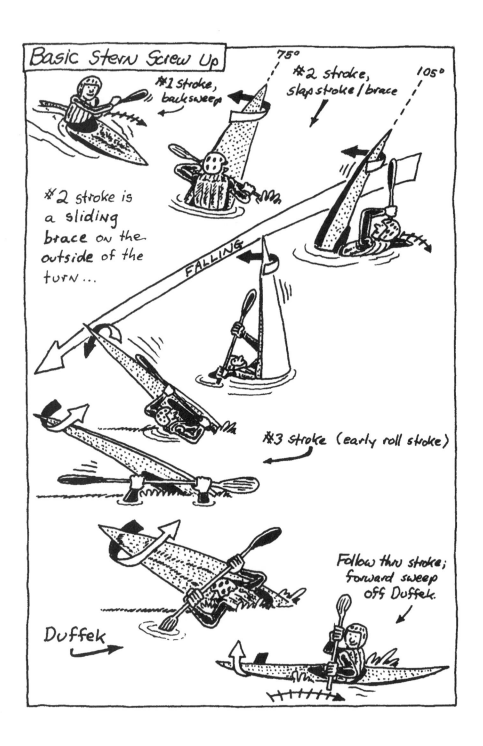

Basic Stern Screw Up

#1 stroke, backsweep

75°

#2 stroke, slap stroke/brace

105°

#2 stroke is a sliding brace on the outside of the turn...

FALLING

#3 stroke (early roll stroke)

Follow thru stroke; forward sweep off Duffek.

Duffek

87

Screw Up Sequence

During a Screw Up, the number-two sliding stroke (a) sends the boat into a backender (b), just before the number-three (Duffek) stroke (c) draws the boat into a spinning exit (d).

when I was on the water with Jeff. I told him how I did this crazy move in my dreams, where I came out of an eddy doing a Stern Squirt in a deep dark valley. I remembered there were some observers standing on a cliff about 50 feet up. I saw them on my original stern-squirt charc as they were about 45 degrees upstream on river right, and I was coming out of the river right side of the eddy. The funny thing was that I maintained a view of them all through the Backender Pirouette. I wondered if such a move was really possible, and Jeff said yes. A half hour of mutual coaching later, the move was real, intact with all the feelings and perceptions I had of it in my dream except, of course, the mysterious observers. So now I just imagine them and watch them in my mind's eye throughout the move.

Mastering the Screw Up means mastering a lot of small points. This should be attempted only after you have attained good control over the position and amplitude of your Stern Squirt. To learn how to do it, the rider must first perform a Backender Squirt. This is focused with the peak point and pulled over backwards with a slap stroke/brace (the number-two stroke of the Stern Squirt technique), done with the blade opposite the backsweep. This is the number-two stroke of the three-stroke combo you must learn for a Screw Up. As you fall over backwards, notice how the original backsweep blade is over your head, as a result of the second stroke. If you were to fall over backwards in this position, the blade is in a ready-to-roll position. Indeed, this is the secret of doing a Screw Up, that you must cheat and do your roll early. Another trick to Screwing up as easy as possible is to let your top weight fall under the boat early in the move, when the boat has attained approximately 75 degrees vertical. By doing this, you skip from 75 to 105 degrees vertical, without going through the degrees in between. Watch the imaginary observers to master this aspect of the technique.

There is an alignment aspect of a perfect Screw Up which is advisable to adhere to. It's a simple concept really and is used to make sure you are synchronizing as well as possible with the local currents. It follows the same principle as the grain alignment technique of simple Stern Squirts going out of eddies—you are trying to have the thin wing sections of the boat cleaving (parallel to) the grain of the current at the peak of the move. Remember that the move peaks with the effort of the number-two forward stroke on the outside of the turn. In this case, however, the boat is peaking at a past vertical station and just for the briefest of moments. You still are using a forward sliding stroke on the outside of the turn and you still are peaking parallel to the grain; you are just past vertical when it happens. Without this alignment you are effectively a dull knife trying to cut across the grain of the currents and you will get less-slick results. Stern Screws are a true test of commitment and energy. You have to approach it with enough energy to send the boat into a vertical Backender. You just short-circuit the process with the Screw technique. If you don't fly into it, you won't fly out.

The Back-Cut Screw Up is a good solid move using a charc that cuts against the whirlpool energies. Any "back-cut" maneuver is done spinning against or in opposition to the whirlpool charcs. For a Back-Cut Screw Up, the squirtist approaches the eddy line with a steep charc and the bow cuts directly back towards the eddy, making the Stern Squirt under, —or against—the grain. The only disadvantage to this maneuver is that, sooner or later, it will leave the boat stalled out on the eddy line. So, leave an exit charc for this situation.

Focus Points
1. Use powerful rounded charcs and activate your rocker.

2. Trip your top weight under the boat when it has attained 75 degrees vertical by throwing your third point to the outside of the turn and up.
3. Use the three-stroke combo: backsweep; sliding support stroke on the outside of the turn; early roll/Duffek.
4. Add some zip to your life by doing a Screw Up lead into a Smash: a Smash Up.

BOW SCREWS

Bow Screws are the bow station version of the Screw Up, which means you are doing a past vertical spin. There are a few helpful hints to consider here. First, you need to make sure you are high enough in your bow station to ensure you will fit "under" your stern as you spin around. This means the boat must be propped up at about a 50- to 65-degree angle. Then use a forward stroke on the outside of your spin to initiate the screw. As the stroke plays out and you go into your spin, take the same blade you stroked with and raise it to near your stern. It helps to align as vertically as possible at this point to get maximum revolution out of the boat. You can do this by looking up, reaching skyward with the "business" blade, and trying to visualize your long axis and keep it aligned vertically as long as possible. As you are going for the exit stroke, which is with the same blade you initiated the Screw with, remember to use the stroke as late as possible and to keep the shaft as parallel to the water's surface as possible. This is because, if you do the stroke early or the shaft is angled to the water, the exit blade will sink deeply and possibly fail and certainly be hard to extract. This is a good stroke to slide instead of just grab for. Sliding the stroke will extend the period of time it can support you and allow you to keep sliding it toward the surface instead of pulling it underwater. It also helps to keep your face low to, or in, the water throughout the finish of the Bow Screw. This allows the water to support your body and helps insure the paddle blade will be as close to parallel to the water's surface as possible. It helps keep you from grabbing for the exit stroke earlier than is necessary, too.

If you need to, while you are learning or in turbulent situations, you can use what is called a "cheater stroke." The cheater stroke is done with the opposite blade than the normal initiation/exit/outside-of-the-turn blade. This means it is the leading, not trailing, blade as you go through the spin.

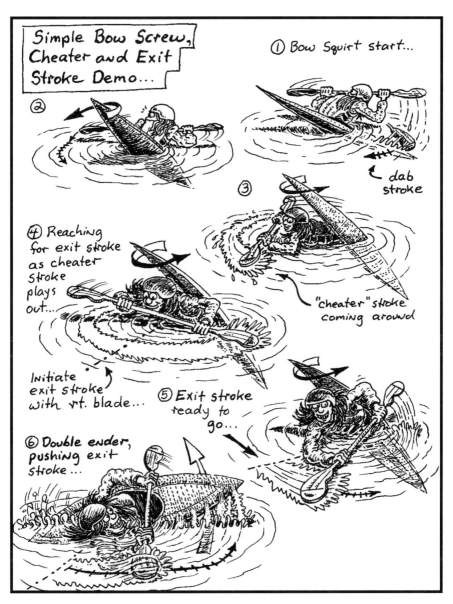

You have to feather the blade angle so it is open to the oncoming water to help it rise to the surface instead of sink. This is helpful because the blade will be closer to the water initially so it requires no setup and essentially doubles the amount of time your blades can support you. You initiate with the outside blade but then immediately look to the other blade for support. Remember to finish the Screw with the traditional outside blade in any case. The cheater stroke

Bow Screws (including cheater stroke)

Wait until the stern is high enough (a). Then, a single forward stroke on the outside begins the screw (b). Raise the initiating blade high and try to align on a vertical center (c). Looking up can prolong your spin time (d). If necessary, the leading blade can be used for a "cheater stroke" (e). The standard exit blade is the same that started the screw; try to keep the shaft parallel to the water's surface and use it as late as possible (f). A small stern squirt is a stable exit to the Bow Screw (g).

often looks a bit forced and grabby but it works.

A low Double Ender is a natural finish to the Bow Screw. If you want more action, read on to the "Screwing Around" and "Washouts" chapters. You can come out of Bow Screws with a lot of momentum and these more advanced techniques are excellent formats to play with that energy. Once you have memorized the stroke sequence and exit stroke placement and technique, your Screw will become automatic. The only thing left to check in each case then is that you are high enough in your bow station to make it work. If you are too low, your body will be swamped in water throughout the move and it will be somewhat slow, wet, and embarrassing. This is another classic squirt technique in that it follows a staccato timing. A slow methodical setup is followed by an instantly flashy and splashy exit.

Focus Points

1. Make sure your stern is high enough when in the bow station.
2. Use the same blade to initiate and exit the Screw—the blade on the outside of the turn.
3. Try to look up and align vertically.
4. Keep the shaft close to parallel to the water and use the sliding exit stroke as late as possible.
5. Use the cheater stroke when necessary.

SCREWING AROUND AND WHIRLYGIGS

When you combine Bow Screws and Stern Screws consecutively you are "Screwing around." To screw around is to do past vertical Cartwheels. Most people start in the bow station as this is the easiest station to attain. As you spin into your Bow Screw exit, normally a low Double Ender, you need to remember to slide your exit/support stroke around the corner of the boat to find support from the "future water." As you are doing this it helps to tighten your abs to dictate the angle of the rising bow so that it goes just past vertical. It also helps to keep your eyes open so you can check the bow's angle in relation to the surface of the water. Remember that as you go to your past vertical station you have a moment's chance to clean and balance your form as you pass through the station. So don't be afraid to stall or slow down for that moment to keep your form clean.

Once you have attained this past vertical stern station you have two choices. One option is to fetch a big backstroke

which will be reached above your head and somewhat deep in the water. The thing to remember for this standard form of screwing around is that you don't want this backstroke to become too involved or time consuming. You can do this by not pulling too hard on the stroke and using weight throws more than the stroke to effect the transition. The other option is to use the other side of the paddle blade to perform a Powerface Smash which creates the form of screwing around

known as Whirlygigs. Whirlygigs are faster, more efficient and dynamic than regular screwing around. To do a Powerface Smash means to effect the Smash stroke with the powerface of your paddle blade instead of the back of the blade as you would do for a backstroke. You have to turn your wrist to open the powerface of the paddle for this maneuver, but it leaves you in a position where it is much easier to slide your blade edgewise through the spin motion you are experiencing. It also leaves the blade much easier to extract once you have attained your bow station. The end result is past vertical Cartwheels which are much faster and possibly lower angled if need be. In fact, a key issue for Whirligigs is making sure your Smashes keep you vertical

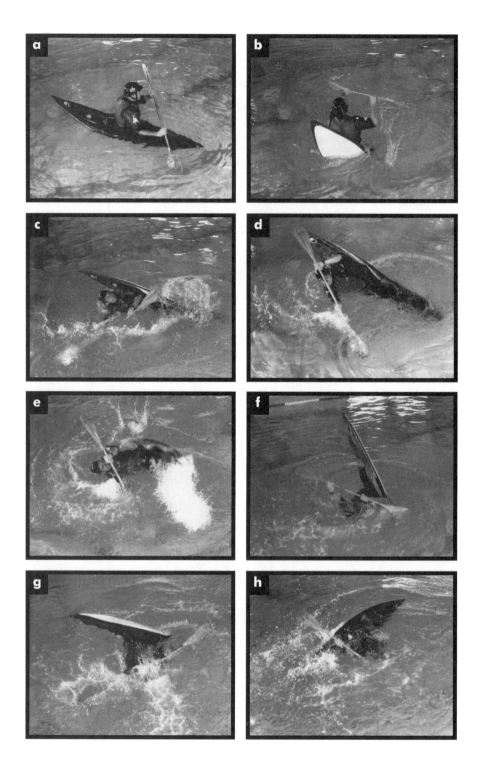

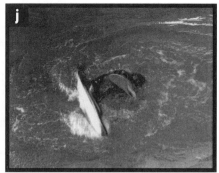

Screwing Around and Whirlygigs

Screwing Around begins with a traditional Bow Screw (a, b, c). But then the exit blade slides under the rising bow to attain a squared-up, past vertical position (d, e, f). This is the defining juncture between a Whirlygig and Screwing Around (g). For the Whirlygig, use a Powerface Smash (h, i) to send the boat into a squared-up, past-vertical bow station, with better body position and the blade in a more releasable configuration. For Screwing Around, a regular Smash stroke using the back of the blade (j, k , l) brings you to a past-vertical bow station, but the stroke is slower and more involved in the water. Both Whirlygigs and Screwing Around leave you with a standard bow screw exit stroke (m), but remember to slide it under the rising bow as in pictures d, e, and f.

enough so the following Bow Screw can be done at a high enough angle. The Powerface Smash will give you total control over the speed and angle of the Smash. I recommend working at just past vertical angles so that you can refresh in your stations. It's possible to do Whirligigs at extremely low angles, and it's not considered bad form to do so, but you get wetter and slower the lower you work and that is how the move can break down. It's also interesting to note that the Powerface Smash is a more static form of the cheater stroke mentioned in the "Bow Screw" chapter.

Focus Points
1. Cue into your stations to check your form.
2. When going from bow to stern station slide the support stroke and keep your abs taut to dictate the angle of verticality.
3. Use the Powerface Smash to spin faster or deal with more turbulent waters.

WASHOUTS

Washouts are a bit difficult to explain but dynamic fun to perform. Technically a Washout is a Bow Screw initiated when the bow is in the air. Normally Bow Screws are started from the bow station but Washouts begin in a stern station. The easiest way to do a Washout is as an exit to a Bow Screw. As you come out of a Bow Screw you are going into a low Double Ender (approaching a stern station) with a good deal of momentum. For an excellent Washout you want to enter this stern station with as much lateral momentum as possible in the form of a head-high Double Ender. You do this by using the Bow Screw exit stroke to add energy to the spinning boat and exiting bow. Once you have thrown into your stern station you are somewhat laid back on the remnants of a forward stroke, which was your exit stroke to the Bow Screw. At this point you will signal your bow to drop by contracting your abs to curl your weight past the center of the boat so you can weight the bow. Ideally you will fly laterally to and through your next bow station by reaching for and fetching the same kind of exit stroke you did for the

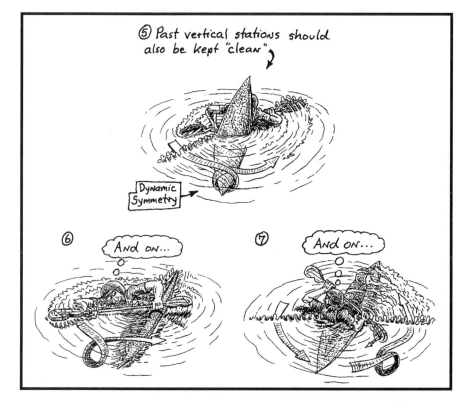

⑤ Past vertical stations should also be kept "clean"

Dynamic Symmetry

⑥ And on...

⑦ And on...

initial Bow Screw with the very same blade. If you fail to make it all the way around and over to fetch this stroke you can always use the Cheater stroke mentioned in the "Bow Screw" chapter. Again, this would be done by opening the powerface and using the leading blade of the spin instead of the standard exit stroke done with the trailing blade. In essence this Washout is a double Bow Screw done with no pause done between the screws. You exit the initial Bow Screw in a low, fast Double Ender and fly through the stern station into the exit stroke for the second Bow Screw immediately.

Consecutive Washouts are an expert maneuver you can learn by slowing the Washouts down and accentuating the

signal for the bow to sink from its mid-air position as you fly past the stern station. As always, it's essential to have clean form in your stations, especially this momentary stern station. By being squared up in the stern station you are in the best position to signal the bow and throw through the Washout. If you need to, when you are learning, there is a very "slow and low" form of a Washout you can do to learn the strokes. Just throw the bow low (about one foot off the water) and lean down hard as you weight the bow to initiate and flow through the second Bow Screw. The problem with this form is that it is so slow and low that it looks pretty boring—and it doesn't leave people guessing how you did it. So, for optimal form,

throw the bow hard and fast into a head-high Double Ender and then throw your body laterally to fetch the same exit stroke again with the same blade.

There are a couple more difficult forms of Washout you can use once you have mastered the standard version. One is a Vertical Washout. To do this you need to leave the initial Bow Screw with the highest possible bow angle. Think of your Screwing Around form to secure this positioning. Once the bow has hit its highest vertical point you throw into the Washout. You will find your body scraping through the water to fetch the exit stroke, but it is quite possible. Use the Cheater stroke if things go bad when you are attempting

Standard Washout

Begin with a standard Bow Screw (a, b, c). Then use the exit stroke to throw the bow laterally very hard (d). Go for another Bow Screw exit, using a cheater stroke if necessary (e, f, g, h). This second Bow Screw exit stroke can end the Washout or send you into multiple Washouts (i).

Vertical Washout

The Vertical Washout has the same Bow Screw initiation as the Standard Washout, but the exit stroke throws you through a perfectly vertical stern station.

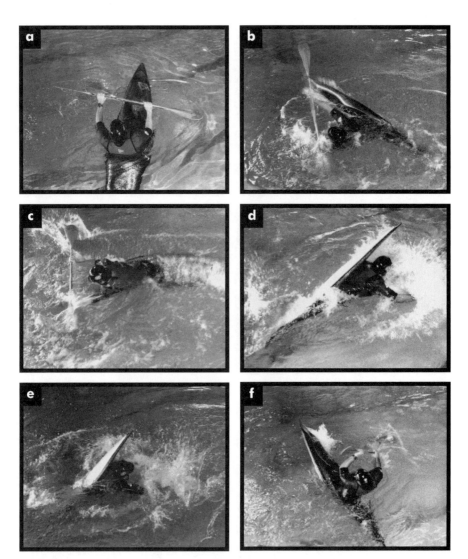

Simple Washout

Unlike other Washouts, the Simple Washout starts with a simple Stern Squirt (a). Level through your stern station before signaling the bow down into a Regular Washout exit (b, c, d). It looks fast and splashy, but you are reaching for a regular Bow Screw exit stroke the whole way (e, f).

this one, although technically this is considered a form break for Washouts. It's also possible to do consecutive Vertical Washouts, but even a few in a row will test your abs to their limit. Remember to demand clean form in your stern stations if you want to do many consecutive Vertical Washouts. This will result in a staccato style where you stall slightly in the stern station and then fly through the bow stations.

The most difficult form of Washout is the Simple Washout. This simple move starts with a Stern Squirt done about head high with the standard backsweep stroke on the inside of the turn. Once in your stern station take a moment to check that you are squared up, signal the bow down, and fly into the exit stroke. This is yet another staccato-form squirt move where the setup is slow and methodical and the exit is blindingly fast. Again, if you have to for learning, do a tame version of the Simple Washout by going slower with the bow lower and then throw your weight onto the bow very hard as you go for the exit stroke. Ultimately this is poor form, however, as it is pretty boring and easily reveals how the manuever is done.

Focus Points

1. Coming out of the initial Bow Screw, throw the bow out to a head-high Double Ender with a lot of lateral momentum.
2. Reach for the standard Bow Screw exit stroke to accomplish the Washout.
3. Use the Cheater stroke if necessary.
4. Consecutive Washouts require cleaning each station.

THE TEST

The Test is a simple but difficult way to test your flatwater skills. It involves all levels of Cartwheels in a single consecutive maneuver, which takes about a minute. You start with two low Cartwheel stations. You then proceed to hit two head-high stations, two past-head-high stations, two vertical stations, two to four past-vertical stations (including Whirlygigs or Washouts if you want), then you retreat to two perfectly vertical stations, two high stations, two head-high stations, and finish with two low stations. It is permissible to stall in the stations for a moment, but it is a form break to hit more (or less) than two stations at any level besides past vertical. The key here, of course, is to be disciplined about cleaning your stations.

Focus Points

1. Clean each station—pause if you have to.
2. Hit exactly two stations at each level, but more past-vertical stations if you want.

The Test

The Test requires a series of Cartwheels through low (a), head-high (b), high (c), vertical (d), and past-vertical stations (e), and then back down through in reverse order.

CUBIC
FREEDOM

ROCKET MOVES

This is a technique in which the rider does a slight Stern Squirt at the base of a wave while moving downstream and proceeds to peak the Stern Squirt at the crest of the wave. This is a proven means for piercing huge holes with control. Easy to perform, it is also a highly photogenic maneuver. I developed and named it on the New River, a perfect arena for squirtech. It's best to learn on relatively small waves,

ROCKET MOVE

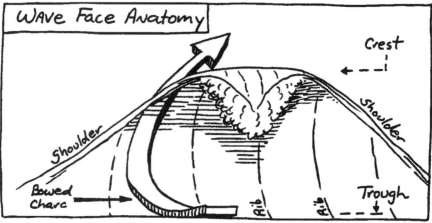

WAVE Face Anatomy

Crest

Shoulder

Shoulder

Bowed Charc

Rib

Rib

Trough

about two feet or less. It can create incredible scenarios like the incident I experienced on the New River on the Fourth of July, 1983. While running Middle Keeney Rapid, I dropped into a large hole a little bit slowly and exited on a Rocket Move. It shot my entire boat clear into the air. Directly downstream in my path lay a five-foot, foamy wave/hole. Worried that I would power slam into the crotch of the hole and do a super-turbo Backender, I actually took a few strokes in midair. To my amazement, my boat flew completely across the trough and landed on the backside of the next hole. My super-soft landing, after a 15-foot flight, left me with my eyes rolling. Although I've tried several times, I've never been able to duplicate the flight. It does give me something to shoot for.

The trick to the Rocket Move is in the approach. You need to develop a bowed charc to establish lateral momentum. The hip of the boat should press under at the base of the wave, lined on a charc that proceeds up the shoulder to the very peak of the wave. There are two ways of actually effecting the Rocket Move. One way uses a backsweep to sink the stern, the other uses a forward.

I prefer the forward-sweep method as it gives a little more control and ability to pierce the foam. Both techniques can leave you vertical at the crest of the wave with your hull side towards the heart of the hole. The idea is to set up a final stroke that will propel you through the foam. The best line will lead you directly up between the foam pile and the shoulder, in order to tap maximum acceleration from the water. As your stern is sunk throughout the move, it is not unusual to nearly backender at the crest. A good exit from this situation is a series of spins, Cartwheels, or a Screw Up leading into surfing position.

Remember that the backside of a large wave is often more troublesome than the upstream face. Coming down

Rocket Move (Side view)

Boosh!

① ② ③

the back of a ten-foot wave can resemble the ride you'd expect from a steep slide. A steep charc will minimize the lateral torque applied to a boat. Otherwise the rushing water can "clip" you from the side and cause you to go for a deep brace. Many times, I've seen someone punch a large hole only to fall over on the backside. This is because they didn't plan their charc all the way through the wave, but only up the face. They find themselves quickly on the backside, falling fast. If their boat is angled, they will be forced to brace. The brace is often eaten up by the turbulent waters. So, remember to keep a steep charc all the way through the wave.

There is such a thing as a Backwards Rocket Move. The rider proceeds backwards down the river, facing upstream, to set up the final stroke. Enter the base of the wave with an angle so that the final backsweep aligns the boat with the grain as it ascends the wave. The boat will crest the wave with the stern piercing the foam and rising straight to the sky. A good follow-up is a Double Ender to Cartwheels. Rocket Moves leave the boat connected to a patch of water momentarily, and so lessens your ability to respond to surprises. Because of this, it is advisable to try them only on wave trains that you know are clear of shallow rocks or pourover holes.

The backsweep technique sets the boat vertical sooner but can leave you more involved in the foam, because it is slower. The slower boat is more subject to the lateral energies of the shoulder of the wave. These energies will set you across the wave into the foam pile. You will probably clear the foam, but exit on a very static charc.

Mainly, I concentrate on setting a bowed charc that will

help my hip bury at the base on a single forward stroke lasting all the way to the peak. I also lean back a bit so the foam will split off my chest. I also premeditate my follow-up. Try to look fast and splashy.

Focus Points
1. Set up a laterally bowed charc that will lead you up the shoulder.
2. Effect the stern-squirt stroke at the wave's base and ride it all the way up.
3. Let the boat turn into the spin mode as it climbs.
4. The boat should point skyward at the crest with half the boat in the air.
5. It is not necessary to enter the wave quickly.

WAVE MOVES

During a surf, the rider seems to go for an Ender but disappears into the wave. He reappears with his bow pointing straight up through the crest of the wave, Backender style. Or he may reappear with his bow pointing downstream, having done a 180-degree spin inside the wave. These are variations of the Wave Move, a dynamic exit from a surf. Jeff Snyder created and developed the Move at Ender Waves Rapid on the New River. One day he just started going for deep-ender charcs, which he would change to a Stern Squirt on exit. Since then, the move has developed into a fine technique with specific steps. It is very similar to the "kickoff" that ocean surfers perform to escape a collapsing wave. In one fell swoop, the boat goes from surfing into a Backender; you can even screw up in time to surf the second wave.

The critical techniques here, as usual, pertain to the approach. As the move will peak in a Backender at the crest, it helps to sink your stern at the shoulder of the wave with a charc that will rebound the boat back to the heart. Cut back and forth on the wave's face and feel for a seam, where it will try to tug your hip under. Set up a charc that will bring you to the seam with some lateral energy. As you enter the area, let your bow pearl as if for an Ender. This helps slow the boat and connects it to a patch of water. It also stores some buoyant energy in the bow, which will help it spring out of the water for the Backender. Let the onrushing water kick the bow back into the heart of the wave as your hip buries deep in the seam. At this point, you will be

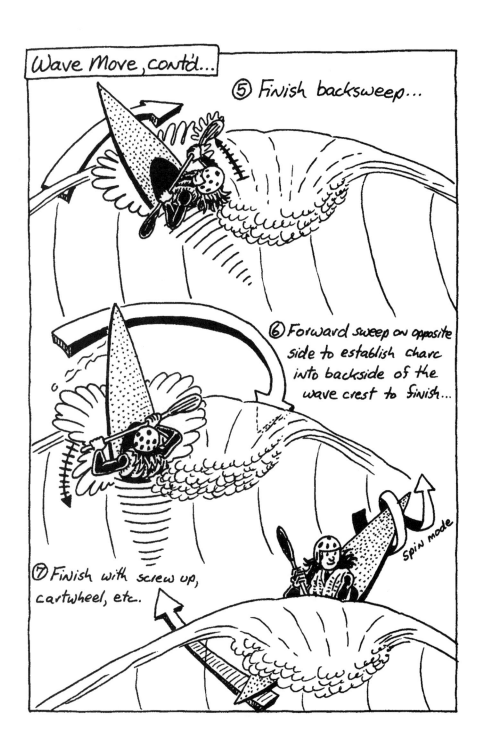

perpendicular to the grain, halfway up the face of the wave. Lean upstream and effect the Stern Squirt with a backsweep on the inside of the turn. This charc sets up the Backender exit, which resembles a Rocket Move. Remember to take your time performing the Stern Squirt and use very bowed charcs with a long slow lean upstream. It helps to have a concise exit to the Wave Move; descending spins are easiest. A Screw Up into a bow upstream mode is a good way to reestablish control and a Smash follow-up can lead to easy Cartwheels done with the grain.

Focus Points
1. Use cutbacks to find the seam.
2. Set up a lateral charc that buries the bow.
3. Halfway up the wave, effect the Stern Squirt.
4. Take your time and use a clean exit.

ROCK SPLATS

The Rock Splat was developed by Jesse Whittemore. It's a popular squirt maneuver in which the squirtist stands his boat vertical, upstream of, or next to, a rock. This move takes a lot of tuning and timing and nerve, so I recommend you make your first few tries in deep, slowish waters, on rocks with consistent pillows and, of course, no undercuts.

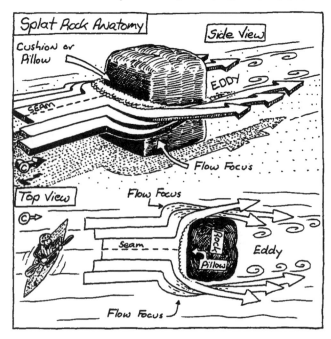

Pick a splat off of the corner of the rock to ensure a safe exit.

Complete the move with a lot of precision, preferably without touching the rock, as this is sure to change your exit charc. Jesse uses a Splat variation called a Smear, whereby he lays his boat on the rock for awhile. Sinking either end of the boat is a good lead into Cartwheels, in front of or next to the rock.

It's best to try your first few Splats on rocks that are low or well rounded on top. Attain a static position next to and just

120

Basic Bow Splat

① Backsweep & sink bow. For a safe bow squirt, keep torso well to either side of seam

② Continue Backsweep...

SEAM

Peak

③ Peak squirt at corner. Forward stroke on opposite side spins boat out and away from rock after move peaks out...

④ Finish spinning into grain, ad lib.....

a bit upstream of the rock. Keep the boat parallel to the grain near the line where the pillow meets the downstream currents. Create a slight lateral charc away from the rock while you set up a reverse sweep between the rock and the boat. When the currents tug your upstream hip under, lean into it and perform the backsweep, which will squirt your stern. Try to gauge how closely your bow will pass near the rock. In the beginning, work a good distance from the rock to assure clearance. It's also smart to do your first few quickly and cleanly, although in time you will be able to park vertically exactly upstream of the rock.

Sinking the bow is a little trickier. Do a backstroke on the upstream side. Lean down hard on the bow and then go for a backstroke which will drive the bow to its nadir. Concentrate on sinking your knees and watch your positioning in reference to the rock.

Body Splats occur when the boat spins and leaves your body between the boat and the rock. These are slightly unsafe because your face can get pressed to the stone and your stern tends to poke under the rock a bit, as if looking for entrapments. Some daredevils even splat undercuts and rafts. Why, I don't know.

If a rock has a huge, inconsistent pillow, you can do a Splat on the corner where the currents turn downstream. Use a lateral charc, with your bow pointing slightly upstream away from the rock. Drop your stern towards the rock as you approach. Spin 270 degrees quickly to face the hull towards the rock as you go around the corner. Make sure it is always deep enough, upstream of the rock.

Focus Points
1. Be picky: choose clean pillows with suitable conditions downstream.
2. Set up a slight lateral charc away from the rock into the pillow's sea.
3. Control your clearance over the rock with lean control.
4. Exit under control.

SWIPES

A Swipe is a simple move I created in 1985. It involves approaching a rock from upstream and effecting a bow pillow squirt, which exits with a fast Double Ender. Both splats barely clear the rock. The move usually throws a splash of

Swipe Sequence

A curved entrance and early bow squirt (a) allow the rider to feel his position on the pillow (b) before the Double Ender (c).

water on the "swipestone." It is photogenic and fun.

Be sure the water is deep enough as this move generates notable torque and you wouldn't want it arrested. Approach the rock slowly and towards its side. Use a bowed charc, which will turn you away from the rock rather early in the game. Well before you encounter the pillow, do a Bow Squirt, sinking the bow under the currents approaching the rock. Let the boat climb to vertical with its stern clearing the rock as you near. As the boat starts to slip around the corner, effect the Double Ender. The bow should pass very closely over the rock and end up pointing downstream or into the eddy. The entire move is done fairly vertical to the grain.

A Swoop is a cubic variation developed by Eric Lindberg. As you leave your Swipe, let your lateral momentum smash the bow into the upcoming eddyline for a powerful entrance to a Mush Move. You can then eddy up underwater, or proceed downstream underwater, or bust a Light Loop. The toughest variation is a Bow Screw Swipe, which is simply a Bow Screw lead into the Swipe exit. Be sure you leave enough room for your body to pass between the rock and boat during the Bow Screw entrance and initiate the Bow

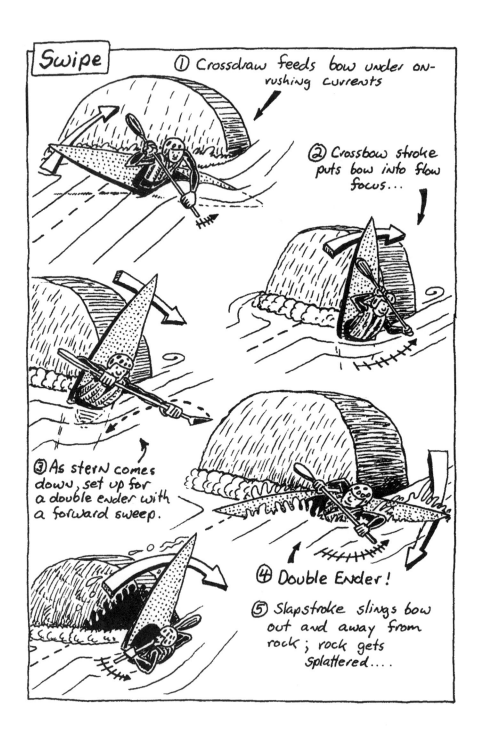

124

Screw quickly to make sure you don't get hung up later. Bored? Maybe you should work on your Bow Screw Swoop Loop!

Focus Points

1. Use deep water and a not-too-vertical rock face.
2. Set up a charc that will veer away from the swipestone.
3. Early in the move use a crossdraw to sink the bow under the currents approaching the rock.
4. As you slide by, perform the Double Ender.

MYSTERY MOVES

The Mystery Move is a form of squirt in which both ends of the boat sink simultaneously. The move and its exit, the Black Attack, are used to explore the depths of large whirlpools under control. Experts can sink to their armpits in flatwater. The move was developed in early July 1985. The move is radical in concept but high in control. Strong eddies, or whirlpools, are required to sink the entire boat and rider. Mystery Moves can also be done as an exit to a surf or a blast with the mover disappearing into the wave and reappearing 20 to 60 feet downstream. The essential trick is to do

Mystery Move Demystified...

It's a flat spin moving thru 3 dimensions!

Flatwater Mystery Move

① Initiate plow squirt sequence...

② Bury bow...

③ Backsweep to sink stern...

④ Level boat underwater, set up for second backsweep...

⑤ Second backsweep, or a forward sweep on the outside of the turn, augers the bow up and out...

⑥ Finish...

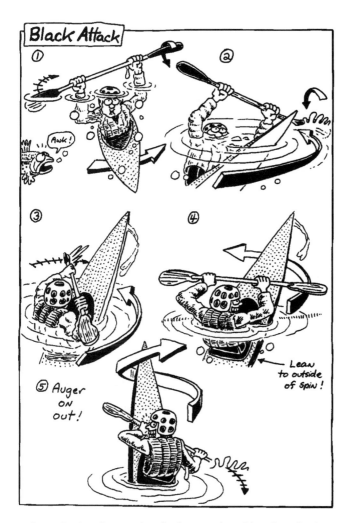

a Stern Squirt after snaring the bow under with a Bow Squirt.

The charcs involved are complex, especially after the rider has sunk out of sight. The easiest way to learn is on flatwater. Paddle forward hard and effect a Plow Squirt. While you still have some forward momentum, do a backsweep or grab a quick forward stroke to sink the stern also. Do the move with the boat as level as possible and accurately determine when your energy has played out, to know when to start your exit. To set up the exit, level the boat underwater and place your paddle in position for a backsweep. This second backsweep pushes the stern to new depths as the bow kicks out skyward at approximately a 45-degree angle.

Doing the Mystery Move as you exit a strong eddy or enter

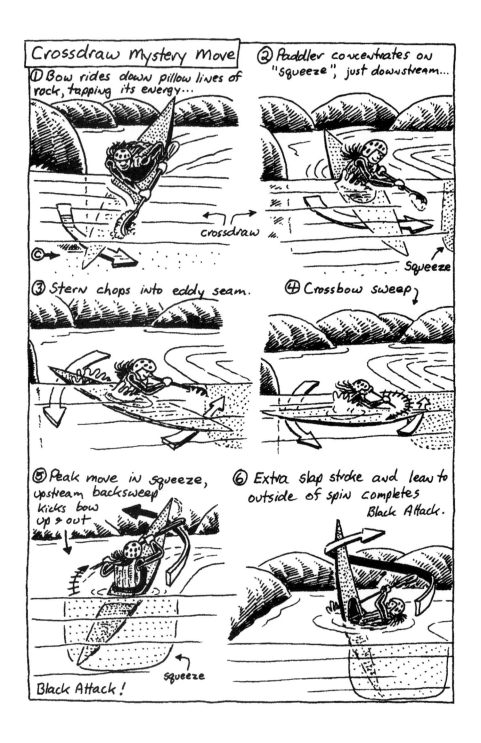

Crossdraw Mystery Move

① Bow rides down pillow lines of rock, tapping its energy...

② Paddler concentrates on "squeeze", just downstream...

crossdraw

©

Squeeze

③ Stern chops into eddy seam.

④ Crossbow sweep

⑤ Peak move in squeeze, upstream backsweep kicks bow up & out

⑥ Extra slap stroke and lean to outside of spin completes Black Attack.

squeeze

Black Attack!

128

a whirlpool is a little more complicated. Use a slight Plow Squirt as a lead into a Bow Squirt, done by a forward sweep on the downstream side. When the forward sweep is completed, the blade is in position to effect the backsweep or a quick forward stroke. Do the Stern Squirt before the bow is facing downstream. Expect the boat to turn quickly back into the eddy and out again, using each new current to sink the boat deeper. Pay attention to the diving angle of the body area of the boat to control the rise and fall at this stage. This works until your upper blade goes underwater, in which case the paddle becomes hard to move. Remember to spin downstream quickly after the bow has sunk. If you're having some trouble learning, leave the eddy with the bow pointing slightly downstream perpendicular to the grain. This sinks the bow easier but robs energy from the stern sink. Always stay on top of the boat and try to keep it fairly level. To sink deeper, however, you must present a diving angle on the bow to any onrushing currents. Try to hook the knees under ever-deeper water but then slide your hip area under the newly purchased water. The main area I focus on is the transition from the knee bury to the hip bury. You must gauge when to level out the dive. If your spin energy plays out without your being level, you won't find the energy to spin into the level position from which to begin your Black Attack. You will just spin up and out with your stern, instead of your bow, pointing up. Essentially, if you don't do the Stern Squirt soon enough, your Bow Squirt will align vertically into a Front Ender in the heart of the whirlpool. If this happens, try to do an effective Bow Screw by reaching around the boat to find a brace, which will make the boat roll early and save you an unnecessary ear wash. If you can't make this move and fall over, remember there is only one good way to roll in whirlpool currents. The currents will actually help the roll one way. So, if it doesn't work one way, try the other.

The Black Attack is a good way to exit a deep Mystery Move with control. Technically, you have to go underwater completely and reemerge on a Screw Up for it to be an official Black Attack. The idea behind the name is that you are attacking the world on your return from the black. If you can perform a good Screw Up, this move will come easy using a backsweep when the boat reaches its lowest level point. Lean back hard on a spinning charc. The boat will leap into the air, doing fast countless spins. As in any whirlpool ride, on exit the focus should be on keeping your bow leading the spin of the boat. If you are whipped into Backender mode,

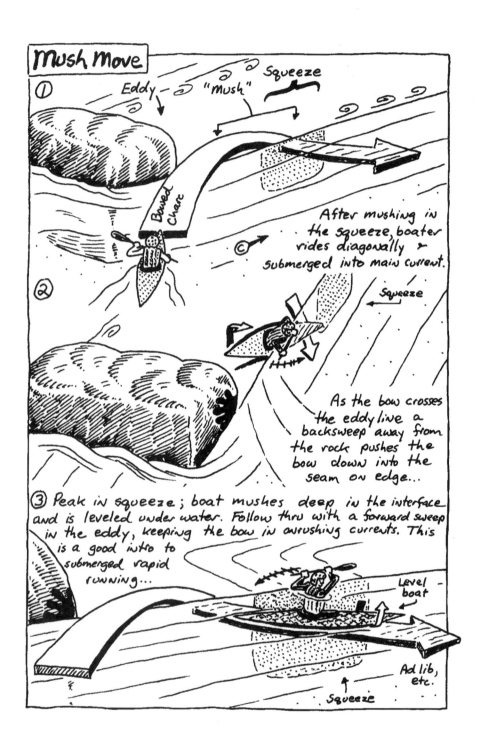

Mush Move

① Eddy — "mush" — Squeeze

Bowed Chare

After mushing in the squeeze, boater rides diagonally & submerged into main current.

② Squeeze

As the bow crosses the eddy line a backsweep away from the rock pushes the bow down into the seam on edge...

③ Peak in squeeze; boat mushes deep in the interface and is leveled under water. Follow thru with a forward sweep in the eddy, keeping the bow in onrushing currents. This is a good intro to submerged rapid running...

Level boat

Ad lib, etc.

Squeeze

use the Screw Up to regain your charc and proximity to air. If you are playing with huge whirlpools, hover in the area where they are forming and when one forms near you, dive your bow deeply into the cone of the heart. Work to level the boat soon, as it will take formidable strength and your blades will be submerged soon. Then read the currents with your feelings and your mind's eye. Apply a diving or rising angle to the outer edge of the boat to rise or fall in relation to the onrushing currents.

Doing a Mystery Move on a wave is fun, safe, and easy. Simply go for a wave move, but bury the bow deep enough to keep it from escaping up out of the top of the wave. Think about the currents deep below the wave currents and visualize a charc that will tap you into them, and pursue it. Try to maintain some spin to add a measure of grace to your exit.

Doing a Mystery Move while blasting is called "subbin'." Set up a lateral blasting charc that will turn back to focus on the heart of the foam pile. As it starts to turn back, lean down on the bow and let it pearl. The rebound should keep the bow turning into very broad charcs until you are perpendicular to the grain and sunken below the foam pile. You will reemerge where the bubbles rise straight up from the bottom of the river. Be careful to work in familiar and safe areas to reduce the risk of your boat catching a protrusion from the river bottom; this could clamp the boat like a paddle flattened down to shelf rock by the currents. Use a backsweep on the inside of the turn for this Mystery Move. If you get stuck to the bottom, wiggle the boat a little, as this will usually let the currents pry under a corner of the boat and lift it quickly to the surface.

Another method of mystery moving on eddy lines involves using a crossdraw Bow Squirt done with the alignment of whirlpool energies, opposite the normal Bow Squirt countercurrent diving method. This develops into a forward sweep on the upstream side, which sinks the stern. The rider must then regroup for the backsweep on exit. This technique lets

Mystery Move

The cross-bow draw becomes a forward stroke which feeds the boat down the pillow lines of the rock.

you start the move very high on the eddy line, where the currents are easy to penetrate. Let the bow start under as high as possible on the pillow of the rock. Make the bow dive quickly to help the stern clear the rock. Think of it as falling off the plateau of the eddy on a spiraling charc that carves back into the eddy. Using a refined version of these charcs, it is possible to mystery move without a single stroke, merely through the power of the charc.

I adapted a variation from the Mystery Move, called the Mush Move. While running downstream past a rock, the Mystery drops you parallel to the grain in the squeeze with a back-cut charc. Approach the rock with a steep rounded charc which veers slightly away from the rock. This is similar to a swipe charc. As you arrive in the squeeze do a strong backstroke on the side away from the rock, which sinks your bow back under the currents just next to the eddy. This is a good entrance to running rapids completely submerged. If you get your chin wet you've attained a "mush mouth." If your head sinks underwater you might get mush for brains. A Mush Move leaves you in a static position underwater. Create your own exit with the buoyant energy you've stored. Remember to roll off the rock's pillow and to drop parallel to the grain with the boat pretty well on edge. Level the boat to secure your position underwater.

Focus Points
1. Visualize a good exit charc in advance.
2. Control the timing of the move by deciding when to level the boat
3. Use a strong, controlled transition from the knee bury

to the hip bury.

4. Keep spinning to set up a good exit charc.
5. Start on flatwater and only attempt to barely sink both ends.
6. Try Mystery Moves in seams in the current. Finish your Black Attack with a Smash—a Mystery Smash Up.

LOOPS

The squirt boating versions of Loops are different from the rodeo move of the same name. Rodeo Loops are a version of an Ender where you flip end for end in the air to the extent that you land on your stern and then hull—basically completing a front-on 360-degree vertical transition. Squirt Loops are done submerged and usually finish off a Mystery Move. They are simply a barrel roll done underwater. There are four types of Loops—Plain, Retarded, Light, and Inverted—which are basically differentiated by their positioning and timing. I started doing deliberate Loops at Twisted Sister (Mystery arena) on the lower Gauley in the fall of 1997 after myself and numerous others had done impromptu ones in various unplanned modes such as running rapids. Retarded and Light Loops were developed in 1999 by myself. Inverted Loops were first done by myself in August of 2000.

Plain Loops are done the deepest of the three. You usually need to attain a Mystery depth of four feet or more for this one (measured from the top of your skirt). For good form (in case someone is watching) you need to remember your ideal positioning for Stern Screws. In Stern Screws you want to time the peak of the Stern Screw, which is when you are past vertical but in your stern station, so that the wing sections of the boat are cleaving the grain of the current. The long axis of the wing section is approaching parallel to the grain. This is similar to the form involved with having the

Light Loop

Two different perspectives on a Light Loop. From a chest-deep Mystery, a sliding stroke launches the bow into a high Stern Screw exit. The boat is best worked at angles about 45 degrees from the water's surface.

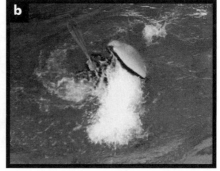

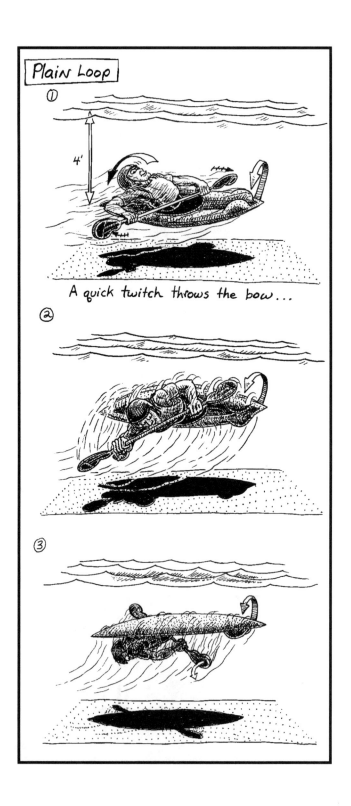

Plain Loop

① 4'

A quick twitch throws the bow...

②

③

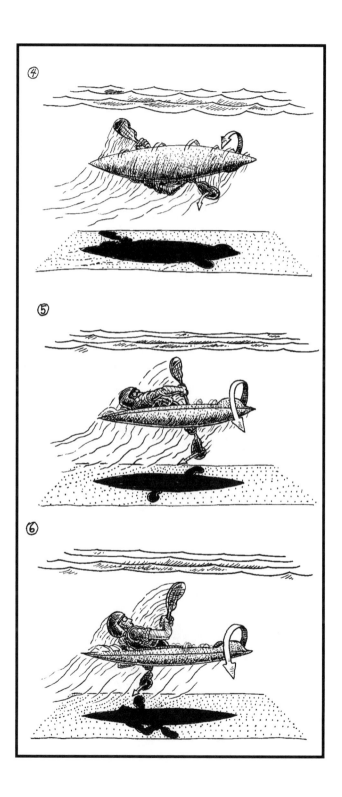

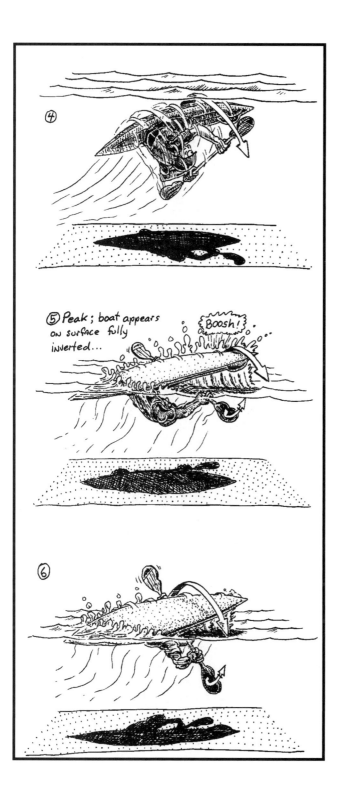

⑤ Peak; boat appears on surface fully inverted...

Boosh!

⑥

thin section of your boat split the currents in your stern station for simple Stern Squirts, but for Stern Screws you are past vertical at this exact moment, and for Loops you are well underwater and describing a cylinder with your boat's carving.

So if you drop in for your deep Mystery with a pretty broad charc, properly, as you drop underwater you are approaching your deepest moment as you close in on parallel to the grain of the current. To loop you send your bow skyward around your deepest point. But you lay back so flat and low that the boat quickly revolves over your head and comes back to square under you in just a flash and totally underwater. This is very easy to do and requires almost no motion by the rider. Perhaps just pointing the chin is all that's necessary. When you are ready to loop, your paddle should be in a perfect position for a backsweep on the inside, or a forward sweep on the outside, of the turn. The same paddle position works for both strokes and you basically do both strokes at once. You can pressure either blade to the same effect. A good time to concentrate is when you hit your deepest point. Look up and throw your bow between your head and the surface. You'll see it flash between you and the light for just a second. Remember to lay back here. It's like your body goes low as your bow goes up. As soon as you witness your bow flash over your head you will find yourself approaching upright with the paddle in the same position as when you started. Just keep the boat flat until you surface. If you have gone deep enough, Double and Triple Loops are fun, easy, and fast, so go for it! You just have to breeze through the leveling-up period after every Loop. Be careful to only try Loops in known, deep areas. It seems there is great potential for whacking your head on a rock at hyper-speed if you work in a suspect arena. It could end up being your last Mystery.

Retarded Loops are done as you are breaking the surface of the water on your return from a Mystery. They can be thought of as a way–past-vertical Black Attack. You need to wait until you are about three feet below the surface and then Loop slowly (with "retarded" timing) so your bow is peaking in its past vertical station as it breaks through the surface. You will then do a standard Stern Screw exit to find yourself level and surfaced. Timing is everything for these kinds of Loops and it seems pretty necessary to keep your eyes open to judge your distance from the surface and therefore your timing. Loops are very easy to do and a successful outcome is almost a given, so concentrate on the aesthetics of your Black Attack. It should be smooth and unhurried but very, very deliberate.

Light Loops apply to the largest number of arenas. They can even be used as exits to Mush Moves. All you need is an initial chest-deep Mystery. You then take a certain stroke to throw your bow into the air at high speed. They are called Light Loops because they make you feel light. One key point to focus on is maintaining a trace of bow speed to feed you through the curvy charcs of this move. As your bow spins to its deepest point of the initial Mystery, maintain a bit of momentum to feed speed into the next section of the move. The only way to do this is to set up this special stroke as you

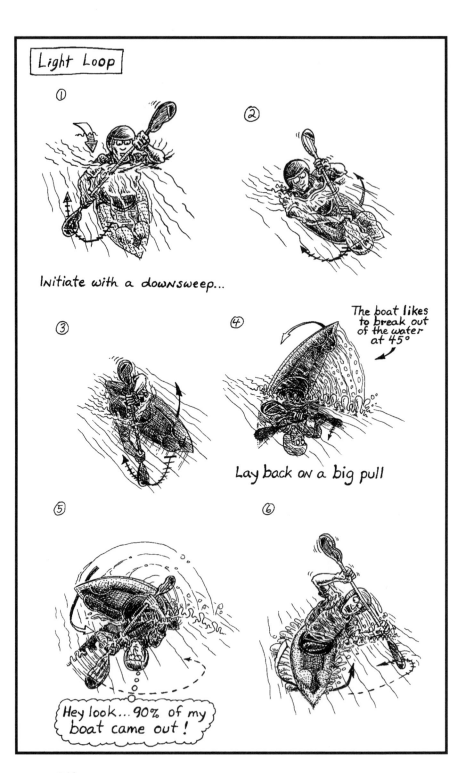

140

are dropping in. It is a forward stroke done with the blade positioned as close to the bow as possible—virtually straight ahead. So you ride through this deepest point of the Mystery—the nadir—with the stroke already set and the bow maintaining speed into the next curl. You then pull hard on the stroke and completely focus on the verticality of the bow launch. It should be past vertical but not a lot. Look for the slipperiest path. It is around 45 degrees to the water's surface. As you launch through past-vertical for this section of the move, lay back on your stern deck to get the bow as free from the water as possible as quickly as possible. You then have to flex your abs and curl bow-ward to complete the move. If you do this with speed and low angles you can create the illusion of your boat breaking free of the water completely. It is, of course, only an illusion. Your body and paddle are still well connected to the water and working hard with a lot of torque. In fact you can light loop too low and end up digging out some very wet exit strokes and looking for all the world like you just did a clumsy roll. In perfect form you can actually get a sense of aid from the buoyancy of the boat. You have to ride a very slippery charc to get this all to work ideally. So look for this curly slick route and lay into it with as much speed and power as you can and you will approach light speed.

One other kind of Loop is an Inverted Loop. This is a Loop done with the bow down. It's a full Bow Screw accomplished underwater. You can achieve this by keeping your bow low throughout your Mystery and then as you start to rise, assume the Bow Screw position with your paddle and fall into the loop. You use your upper blade to complete this Loop the same as if done at surface level. Remember to cue up to your bow station to complete the Mystery with good form. You will break the surface with your bow slightly deep but level in your station. Perhaps the future holds Retarded and Light Inverted Loops.

Focus Points
1. Loop at exactly the right moment and depth to get consistent results.
2. Focus on the nature and speed of how your bow passes over your head.
3. Loop safely. If you hit your head at this speed, you won't remember a thing.

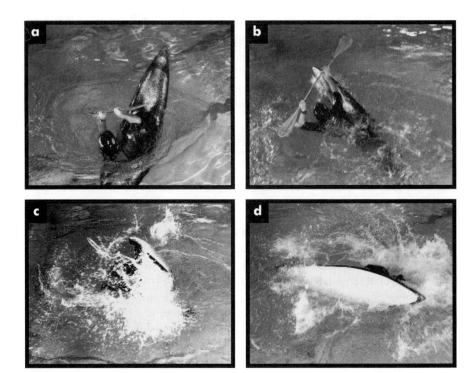

Bow Draw

A bow draw guides the bow from a Mystery and temporarily supports it through a "Flying Washout" of sorts. Upward sideways momentum is key.

FLYING FISH

This is likely to be the most dynamic squirt move. It was first performed by a Japanese paddler named Kuma on the Nagara River in Japan at a Mystery arena named the "Hideaway." He slowly disappeared on a Mystery Move in crystal clear waters. Then he suddenly exploded into what looked like a powered-up Retarded Loop which was so dynamic he acutely cleared the entire boat into the air by 15 to 18 inches. At the peak of the move, his boat was upside down with only his head and the tops of his shoulders in the water. His boat was perfectly parallel to the surface of the water and airborne. He flew. Technically this move is not a Loop. Kuma said he felt he was doing a super Mikawa Attack, which is often considered a "mistake" exit to a Mystery in Japan. The nature of the move is complicated but not inexplicable. It has to do with supporting your body at the crux. You start this move by exiting the Mystery bow up with some spinning speed. As the bow clears into the air you throw into a Bow Screw exit to the inside of the turn. Kuma says you can preface this throw with a bow draw on the inside of the turn and then use the other blade to fetch the Bow Screw exit stroke. It is this stroke which supports the

142

body. Reaching for a Bow Screw with your bow starting in the air is in the realm of Washouts. But this maneuver circumvents the obligatory Smash involved in Washouts. Instead of smashing underwater the bow stays airborne and parallel to the surface of the water. The bow hangs in the air while the stern releases from the water. You finish by completing the flip in the air and you end up upright. There is a lot of energy in this maneuver and I can only speculate that this will play out into even more cubic adventures in the future. Kudos to Kuma.

CLUING

It was bound to happen. After dipping into thousands of Mysteries, finally I've discovered a clue: a thread of alignment that will lead you into or out of Mysteries. Although a good Clue will help your progress on Mysteries, beware. I've found that too many Clues can be as confusing as too few. Put briefly, Cluing is a technique for surfing, in a sustained manner, with both ends of the boat underwater. There are many factors to harness, including a new force: "up" energy. Cluing, as I've learned it, is an incredible, though nonspectacular, technique. Since most of the action is underwater, it is not a real eye-catching event, unless you are a fish. It is a highly entertaining move for the cluer nonetheless.

Clues are limitless and can be found anywhere. To learn, start in a small blasting hole. As you blast, inspect the greenwater slab pouring over the rock. Notice its shape peculiarities and how they align with the sweet spot or shoulders of the hole. Try to picture your bow pinched into

Cluing

the heart of the slab, hovering in the three-dimensional arena between the rock and sky. The boat is hostage to four forces which the rider uses to navigate: up, down, left, and right. The boat is the centerpiece of a compromise between these forces and your will to mingle. The only way to crash such a powerful party is to create your own invitation. They must let you in. Cluing is a very careful piece of time and work spent, and so is much safer than many other high-velocity maneuvers. So you may as well learn to be careful at the outset by carefully selecting your access to this three-dimensional surfing mode. The most inviting access is on the shoulder of the hole. Similar access can be found on the shoulders of "ribs" in the greenwater slab. The idea is to charc slowly up or out the shoulder, but then stall. Try to execute a very slow cutback and lean down on the bow, picking under the surface of the greenwater slab pouring over the shoulder of the rock. Use a slight upstream tilt and a backstroke on the upstream side to pull the bow towards upstream.

Once the bow is under, you've trapped your "up" energy. Your bow is trying to cut back but is actually held like a wing in a strong, thin cross section of flow. You must gain your "wings" in this easy access mode. Learn to use hip tilt to make the bow rise or fall. Blasting techniques can be used to deal with your lateral position in the hole. Always stay well grounded by keeping a major portion of the boat connected to the sweet spot in the foam pile. This guarantees enough energy will be available to pit against the slab currents. Notice how the situation won't let the boat rest. This is mostly because of the up energy. It will pop the boat to the surface at the slightest opportunity. Forward and backward leaning, combined with hip-tilt dynamics, help you guide this energy to keep it subdued beneath a film of water.

Sooner or later, you will have to clue into a complete cutback, underwater, of course. The bow will zoom laterally over the crest of the rock without touching it or popping into the air. If you stall on the cutback with a steep charc, the boat will probably surface into a blasting mode, and you will have lost your Clue.

Be ready to deal with the opposite shoulder of the hole by the time you get there. There are idiosyncrasies inherent in every shape of shoulder. To keep your bow pearled, you must clue into a cutback before you are too high on the shoulder. The easiest Clue is always when the bow is broad charced, about 45 degrees to the current. This keeps the "wing" concept intact. You can clue with steeper charcs. You need to focus on the up energy and where it can go. Try to balance the up impulse between the bow and stern to keep the boat from piercing up through the grain. Remember to keep the effort on your part to a minimum. There is no way you can do battle with these currents, and so you must seek cooperative methods. If it seems to be a lot of work, you

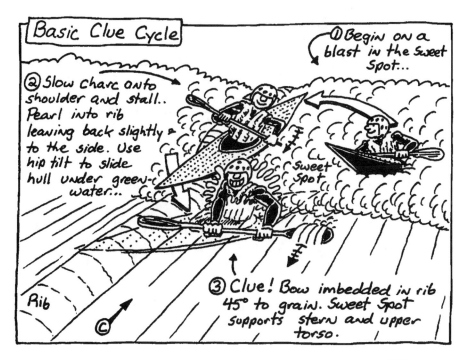

Basic Clue Cycle

① Begin on a blast in the Sweet Spot...

② Slow charc onto shoulder and stall.. Pearl into rib leaving back slightly to the side. Use hip tilt to slide hull under green-water...

Sweet Spot

③ Clue! Bow imbedded in rib 45° to grain. Sweet Spot supports stern and upper torso.

Rib

Cluing is literally weaving the boat into greenwater laminations...

Sweet spot

Rib

have the wrong Clue. Listen to the river and it will show you where the boat can hover effortlessly, completely submerged. I call this experience "boating without gravity."

Before long, you will discover how well cluing works for entry into Mystery Moves. This is because cluing can give you long charcs in a short arena. That is, you can get the angle for the spiral descent much easier when you approach on a line derived from a more three-dimensional format. You don't lose any energy, or charc, breaking the bonds of the second dimension. Those bonds were carefully disassembled when you entered the Clue.

Where Clues lead, I don't know. They are the first step into moves done completely underwater, and with control, for a sustained period of time. The energy of the river can be directed to keep a boat submerged yet safe.

Focus Points
1. Small pourovers are the best arena.
2. Use a slightly oblique angle from a stationary surf to initiate the Clue.
3. Sit upright to help keep the bow's buoyancy trapped.
4. The Clue will probably move, so be ready for cutbacks.

MELTDOWNS

A Meltdown is a move often done uwittingly by beginning squirtists. Perfected by Jeff Snyder, it is usually performed on medium-sized pourovers (one to four feet high). The rider slips over the rock and melts down into the foam on a line leading under the foam to the point where the bottom currents boil up—many feet downstream from the melting point.

Anyone can find the nerve to drop deeply over a pourover, of course. The trick is to stay oriented and under control. This control can be used to achieve a dramatic rocketing exit. With only two major fields of current to deal with—the foam and the bottom currents—the orientation comes from feeling out your position as you pass under the foam. You are traveling on the greenwater slab, and can sense when the boat is starting to lift. All control comes from your entry charc. To embed the boat in the greenwater slab, you need to pick your bow deeply under the foam. As your chest is hitting the foam, lay way back to engage your stern and level out the bow's dive.

You can learn the charcs for this technique quite safely by branching out from your Mush Move charcs. Think of it as a Mush Move done on a completely submerged rock. Jeff recommends the rider be ready to spend several seconds underwater and be prepared to Screw up if the exit is past vertical. As with any totally-underwater maneuvers, the rider should work in familiar waters with minimal hazards downstream from the working area. The exit of a Meltdown is testament to the control of the entry. Good Meltdown technique could save you a gnarly Blast someday, if you find yourself inadvertently running a nasty pourover with your name on it. Just think deep thoughts and then "go towards the light."

Focus Points
1. As you enter the foam of the pourover, pick your bow deeply under the foam by leaning forward.
2. As you pass below the foam pile, determine when the boat's dive has reached its lowest point; then lean back hard to set up the exit.
3. To avoid recirculating, reemerge at the crest of the foam pile, pointing downstream.

SHOWBOATING

THE PEPPER PRY

This flash move was invented by Dr. Don Pepper of Friendsville, Maryland. He developed this radical-looking approach to a Stern Squirt in about five minutes in a pool one winter. You use a normal Stern Squirt charc, essentially, but just before you encounter the eddy line, you drag your paddle near the stern, with its powerface forward. This looks and feels a little clumsy in the beginning, but quickly turns dynamic as the boat spins 180 degrees and the stroke suddenly becomes a Duffek. The blade actually stays motionless on the eddy line while the boat spins 360 degrees around it, at a high rate of speed. The final effect is like that of a kid running down a street, hooking one hand on a pole, and swinging around it. This looks like it could dislocate your shoulder early in the move, when you are trying to nudge your hip under. This segment of the squirt is relatively brief and leads to a segment of super-alignment during the Duffek.

The Pepper Pry should be learned on flatwater, and then on small eddy lines, since your first few attempts will look quite uncoordinated. Set up a super-bowed charc. As the veer is peaking, set up the drag stroke. Use it for a slight brace as you press your hip under. You should lean to the inside of the turn for stability, but tilt the boat to the outside to make the hip bury. Pull the drag stroke forward into position for a Duffek. About halfway through the turn, the blade should be near the bow and you can pull on it slightly to maintain your spin for the final 180 degrees. If you attempt this on an eddy line, make sure the stern is well sunk before it encounters the eddy currents, or they may tip you. Depend on the push you receive from the eddy currents to send the boat back into the downstream currents. The Stern Squirt should lift the bow to around head level—anything higher

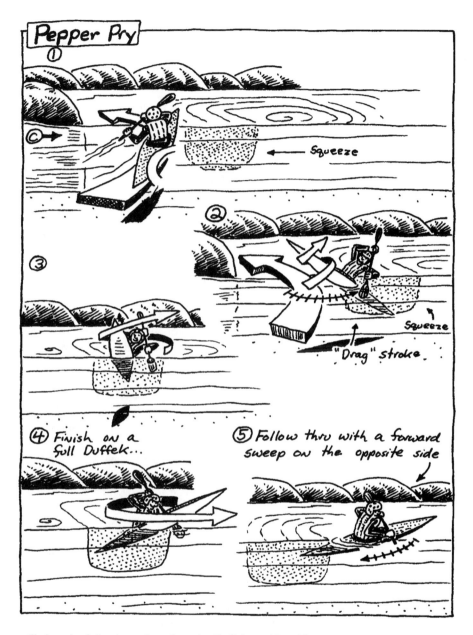

Pepper Pry

① Squeeze

② "Drag" stroke Squeeze

③

④ Finish on a full Duffek...

⑤ Follow thru with a forward sweep on the opposite side

will slow the full spin and confuse the Duffek position. The veer charc is essential to the spin mode.

I consider this a classic squirt move because, like all the others, it starts out looking like a mistake and ends up looking dynamic. It also has a good feel to it. Beginners make this simple move look difficult while experts make it look easy.

1. Set up a veer charc that sinks the stern before it encounters the eddy.
2. Drag the backsweep blade with the powerface forward.
3. Try to keep the spin from slowing down by pulling back on the Duffek.
4. Keep bow only head high.

TWIRLS AND THROWS

While "twirls" and "throws" have been a part of the hot-dogging scene for more than a decade, they are usually done spontaneously in the manner of a foolish fling, so to speak. There tend to be two kinds of throws: the type you catch and the type you don't. This chapter will discuss controlled throws (our helmets cover everything necessary to deal with uncontrolled throws). While the exact origin of the concept of throws is vague, it is probable that the technique began nearly simultaneously in several parts of the country, around 1971 or 1972. I have a limited perspective on the entire arena of this subject, and so will just relate the origin of moves that have remained popular in this region. Incidentally, throws are not entirely accepted here or anywhere. It can be foolish to throw away a perfectly good paddle in a rapid, so my first advice pertains to the proximity of the throw.

The river should dictate the area and timing. All fancy throws and twirls are really just a demonstration of charc, and charc is river-dependent. If you really want to catch the paddle, you must be able to throw with proper anticipation. If you are in surging or irregular waters, you will have difficulty planning the exact landing spot for the stick. On the other hand, the relatively small area required to complete a throw can be found almost anywhere. The focus should be

The consequences of an ill-conceived throw...

on the area in which you will be when you catch the paddle, and what you will do with it once retrieved. Obviously, it helps to use a practiced throw that you can trust to land consistently. The following is a review of such throws and twirls.

The Basic Twirl

The Basic Twirl involves rolling the stick down and away from yourself. Start with the Hand Twirl. With lower arms extended and palms up, tilt your forearm down and let the stick roll to your fingertips. When it reaches them, flick it back to your palms. Repeat the twirl rhythmically and smoothly. Try to minimize the "hop" time, when you lose contact with the paddle. This is a good limbering-up exercise, useful for displaying that nervous, fluttering feeling you get before a run. Learn to toss the paddle to the crook of your elbows and let it roll down your entire forearm. This twirl is faster and displays more energy. It is a high-control move, as long as you are careful that the blades do not contact the water.

The maximum version of this twirl was created by Dan Demaree. Throw the paddle to your elbows and let it roll down. In the last seconds, however, raise your arms until the spinning paddle reaches your fingertips at a position over your head. Then, by inverting your wrists and leaning way back, the paddle spins down the inside of your arms to contact your chest. As it continues down your chest, scoop your arms around and under the descending stick, catching it near the elbows to reestablish scene one. The final effect is that of the paddle spinning around the perimeter of a three-foot cylinder of motion, directly in front of you, contained on the outside by your arms. This can be done in your boat on the water. Be careful that the paddle is centered on your chest on its way down. If it goes off center, one blade may dip in the water and make it look like you

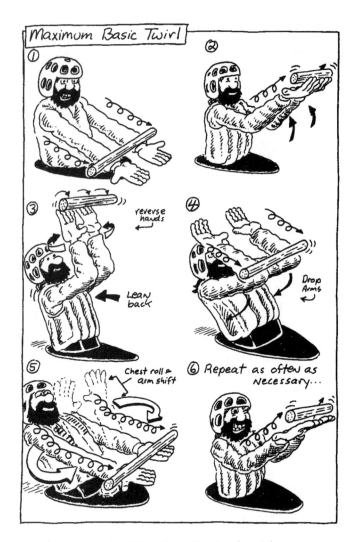

Maximum Basic Twirl

① ② ③ reverse hands ④ Drop Arms — Lean back ⑤ Chest roll & arm shift ⑥ Repeat as often as necessary...

need more practice. Hoop it up. Tossing the stick over your head and catching it behind your back makes a nice finish. Toss it so that it comes down very close to your back, so as not to overthrow your reach. Another version by Dan is "walking" the paddle on your forearms by tossing the blade to each elbow alternatively. The paddle will spin in diagonal patterns, meeting one wrist on one side as it hits the elbow on the other side.

The Schnitzel

A relatively safe move developed by myself, the Schnitzel applies to a wide variety of situations. It can be done as a

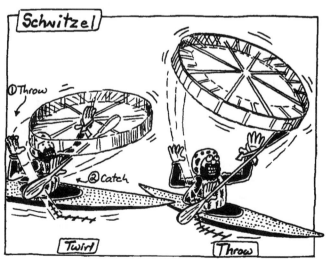

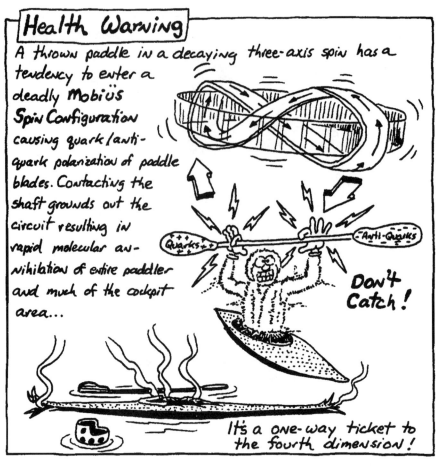

twirl or a throw. It's best to learn the twirl version first. While taking a forward stroke, move your high (pushing) hand to a point just above the center of balance in the paddle. As the low blade exits the water, use your low hand to continue the arc of the blade up and over (around) the high hand. The paddle does a 360-degree spin around the centered hand at an angle approximately 45 degrees to the water. This is a very high-control move and works well against a head wind, or while surfing. This twirl is also a good lead into a Duffek, while fooling with eddies.

The throw version of the Schnitzel is radical-looking but safe because the paddle lands in perfect position for the next stroke. Learn to do the twirl version with a little hop or toss around the high hand. Let the hop get higher and take longer. After a while, you should be able to throw the stick so that it spins in the air at a 45-degree angle and lands back in your hands diagonally ready for a stroke or Duffek.

As in all good throws, you need to concentrate on the throwing hand, not the stabilizing, or "holding," hand. Be sure to toss the paddle high enough to clear over the bow deck as it spins in its diagonal fashion. If you are moving downstream, remember to throw the paddle out ahead of yourself, so it will land where you will be, not back where you were. Another good rule of thumb is to never throw the paddle towards the sun. You may hurt your eyes looking into the sun, which can have an immediate, negative effect on your ability to retrieve the paddle.

A Tilla

This is our name for a move popular everywhere. It requires rolling the paddle around the back of the neck and retrieving it in some usable manner. The simplest way to do one is to start with the low blade, just as it completes a stroke. The low hand lifts the blade into its arc around the neck before it releases the paddle. After throwing the blade, the low hand reaches across your chest, near your neck, and accepts the

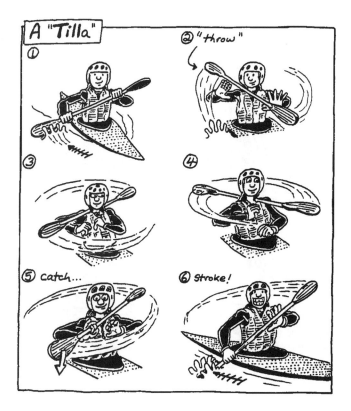

A "Tilla"
① ② "throw"
③ ④
⑤ catch... ⑥ Stroke!

paddle a second after your other hand releases it. This is a good move in a variety of areas, but take care that your blades don't hit the water—like the wave you're surfing—or the stick will exit your scene. It also helps to lean, or duck, halfway through the move. This technique lets gravity help the paddle roll consistently around the back of your neck. Try to minimize the amount of time the paddle is out of your hands. A fancy version of a Tilla is to let the paddle spin down your arm after it has circled your neck. Make sure the paddle is centered on your arm and that you're not wearing a slippery paddling jacket. A Super-Tilla happens when the paddle spins not only around your neck, but also around your arm as you catch it. A version I created is a way to show the space required for most squirt moves, called the Spacemaker. As the paddle comes around your neck, grasp it firmly near the throat. Finish the spin by swinging the stick at arm's length around your space. This really impresses people to respect your space. It's best to use this as a lead into a Duffek.

Hunning

This is a state-of-the-art twirl, developed by Attila Szilagyi. This twirl is done between normal forward strokes. The

blades do a full spin backwards, reflecting sun from the blades, which can be seen as flashes as far as a mile away. The move is done simply but requires supreme concentration to maintain for any length of time.

As your low hand pulls the blade from the water after a stroke, align your thumb parallel to the shaft. As the hand comes up, to become the high hand for the next stroke, you effect the "flick." The shaft spins in your hands, with the top spinning back towards you. Maintain contact with the "flicking" hand throughout each stroke to maintain full control. I subconsciously count the bumps made by the shaft's oval as it spins through the hand, and grasp after the second bump to brake the spin. The paddle should finish its spin as it enters the water.

This is a move that makes people wonder what you are doing, especially if you muff it. As failure will leave you in poor control, try this move in areas where you have a margin for error, like flatwater. You will find that it helps to slow your paddling pace to cover for the extra time it takes to complete the backspin, between each stroke. The move ends up looking laid-back and flashy at the same time.

The Full-Spin Throw

The paddle is thrown ahead and above, spinning end-for-end 360 degrees, in a plane parallel to the water level. Concentrate on the throwing hand. With a little practice, this is a very high-control move, landing surely back in your hands. It can even be done while surfing. If you are throwing the stick while moving downstream, remember to toss the

Full Spin Throw

② Catch

① Throw *

* See "Health Warning"

stick to your future position. This is an excellent throw with which to exit an eddy.

FLINGS

Flings are a foolish affair. They consist of a paddle throw done in mid-Bow Screw, and caught of course. If you do it right you will catch it right as you are about to need it for your exit stroke. If you do it wrong you will catch it on the back of your head as you struggle through the exit with only your hands. There are a few clues to instruct the hapless victims of this technique. The first hint is that you should work pretty close to vertical. This gives you a trace more time and forgiveness on your exit. It also keeps you from traveling too far from the drop zone where you expect your paddle to land. I find it helps to flow into the move without a lot of hesitation in the bow station. This sets up a timing where it is easier to deal with the window of opportunity for throwing your paddle. So drop the bow smoothly to a deep bow station and use the single initiation stroke on the outside of the turn to start the Screw. Then take the blade you just did the stroke with and throw it skyward pretty much into a vertical

Fling

From a bow deep station and a final stroke on the right, throw the paddle up over your right shoulder (a) to the future landing zone somewhere to your left (b, c). You catch it just in time to secure your exit stroke (d).

spin above but slightly behind yourself. You want it to land near where you are about to spin over to. As you throw the paddle, you are starting to spin to the inside of the turn, looking up. You'll probably have to reach a bit to retrieve it and then pull it in for some semblance of an exit stroke. You don't need much help from it really, but to ace the move, you should try to catch it in perfect position and feather for an effortless and graceful exit. Some things to watch out for are to *not* throw the paddle too far away (it's easy to do), and to *not* hit the upright stern of your boat as you throw the paddle. This trick is not a survival skill by any means and should be avoided at all costs—unless you have to show off and are sure you can pull it off. You really look dumb if you blow this one. It's a pretty lame way to get attention.

Definitely wear your helmet to practice this and avoid anyone watching you if possible. If anyone asks why you are doing this, you won't have a good answer. Flings should be kept pretty private, really.

Twizzlin

Twizzlin is another technique best done in private. It has to do with maintaining a prolonged Bow Screw with stirring strokes. This could conceivably result in bow dervishes given optimal conditions and technique. The stirring stroke is by necessity consistent and prolonged. I know of two which work, but I suspect there are more.

The first Twizzlin I developed using a single stirring stroke done in front of your belly as you sit high in a bow station. A backstroke starts you into a vertical spin by pushing away from and across your belly and when it plays out you pull it back to your belly to regain stability and then whisk it thin-wise across the front of your belly to regain the starting backstroke. It ends up being somewhat circular as the backstroke plays out and is then retrieved and replayed. It helps to choke up on the stick so you are working with minimal blade in the water. Squirt boaters with hand paddles can do this maneuver automatically by using both hands and maintaining spin and stability at the same time.

Another technique I developed uses a single trailing stroke. This technique makes you bob up and down in the water in a vulgar manner as you spin. You start comfortably in a bow station and fetch a forward, but down-pulling stroke to start the spin. When the stroke plays out, as you reach your deepest point, you reverse the upward pulling

Twizzlin is maintaining a spinning bow station by means of a continuous stirring stroke in front of your belly.

orientation of the blade and use the powerface side of the paddle to push downward and around, making the boat bob back up. When the "up" stroke plays out and you are at your highest point you spin the blade to set up the upward-pulling "down" stroke. So you spin around in a circle, consistently bobbing up and down. It's nearly shameful and you should only practice this if you are bored AND alone. Think of the consequences if someone saw you fall over trying this. You'd have to say you were *trying* to do that. It's unbelievable. I only developed this in the hope of attaining Bow Dervishes someday, like a skater spinning a pirouette in the center of a big whirlpool. This could be one of the gifts this sport holds in its future.

Dervishes

Dervishes are consecutive vertical, and slightly past-vertical, tight spins. Bow Dervishes have yet to be realized but can possibly be attained with Twizzlin strokes, or just really fine balance, or with hand paddles in a whirlpool. I'd say a true Dervish would have to equal at least three 360-degree spins and a clean exit done blindingly fast.

Many people have done Stern Dervishes although these are not aggressively pursued. This is the equivalent of consecutive Stern Screws done as vertical as possible. A good way to go into a Dervish is with low speed so you don't travel far into the currents and so you maintain a chance of tapping whirlpool energies. Drop into a very vertical Stern Screw position and remember to **not** lay out on the screw much and make it drop low. You need to leave the screw with the sliding stroke on the outside, making efforts to regain your verticality for a second. Once completed, you will find yourself in a somewhat compromised stern station, somewhere near vertical. You now need to clear your blade and launch into the outside stroke of a second Stern Screw. If the boat is only vertical or not even so, throw into a past-vertical Screw position anyway and recover by having the stroke prop you up near the end. The end result looks like a bunch of Screws linked closely with a bounding outside stroke. If you use this technique with fine vertical form and relaxed pacing you can sustain many, many turns that whip around real fast. Hence the name. You may get a little low on control and travel a bit doing this, so make sure the eddy line is not too crowded when you try it.

SOME FLASH STROKES

These are for the "Kill me now, cause I'm bored outta my gourd" club. They are designed to put some flash in your splash. Proceed with caution, because you control the horizontal, but they control the vertical. These are bad-boy moves and you should be punished for trying them. The only prerequisite necessary is a camera on shore.

The Green Lean

This stroke is by far the simplest and most sane one of all: doesn't even leave the rider in jeopardy. This means it's a good stroke for wimps and sissies. On exit from an eddy,

take your last forward stroke on the upstream side. Then, cross your low blade over the stern deck to effect a rudder on the inside of the turn. It helps to choke both hands up to the bow-end blade and hold the stroke for a long time. As in all trick strokes, the idea is to set up a charc that will carry the boat through the move without the help of the flash stroke. The strokes are really just window dressing on the charc, and they demonstrate the power of your charc and balance.

The Backracker

Tired of expensive chiropractor bills? Here's a new twist in backbreaking fun: the next best thing to pushing the panic button. It was developed by the originator of the Green Lean, Greg Green. It is relatively unused but can spice a Class II hole up to a VI, right behind your back.

As you leave a hole, at the shoulder, let the downstream currents draw the bow downstream, until you are in position to backender, if you're in a big hole. Now, apply a Green Lean, crossing a blade over the stern deck, which will attach to the downstream currents just to the side of the hole. You pry the paddle off your backbone and the boat does a dramatic spinning exit. Some paddlers even throw in an impromptu roll. Make sure you are on your way out of the hole or you will practice your behind-the-back roll in the hole itself—quite challenging. The disadvantage to this move is the difficulty in retrieving your paddle if the boat goes vertical.

Perfect form in a
Shudder Rudder
requires a straight high
elbow and a rider looking
downstream.

The Shudder Rudder

This move is even functional! It is a steering mode for surfing or blasting. Find a consistent ride near the base of the
wave and lean way back. Work a light rudder closer and
closer to the stern. At a point where you will be stable for a
second, let the rudder enter the wave above and directly
behind you. The blade remains aligned vertically in the grain

of the current and you apply pressure, left or right, as needed. Lean way back and use waist gyrations to pressure the
blade one way or another. You can even lean back so far
that you are looking downstream, seeing the world upside
down. Try to work lightly and stay over your boat, ready to
recover to a normal surfing mode if need be. You can use
the inverse of this alignment for backblasting. Be careful not
to flip, laid back on the deck, because you will be subject to
an ignoble nosewash.

The Supermove

This was developed by Jesse Whittemore early in his squirt
career. Use a fast broad charc entering an eddy. As the boat
begins to turn, let the upstream hand loose of the paddle so
you can do a one-handed crossbow pry off the downstream
side of the bow. Hold your free (upstream) hand high and
wave to the camera. The holding hand should keep the
paddle at about 45 degrees to the water, with the blade just
in front of the foot area. What a picturesque way to flip. You
can spice this up by leading in with a Schnitzel. This move is
not for namby-pambies. Do it with authority or not at all.

Moonstroking

Someone had to try it. Another seemingly simple but difficult
move. This is very low control and generally applies to areas
of flat currents.

Paddle the boat quickly backwards and downstream, and
then go into the Moonstroking mode. Turn your blades
edgeways as they enter the water, so they cut through with
minimum resistance. Simulate slow forward strokes as you
speed backwards. Lean forward and pretend you're very
late, but paddling molasses. It's a weird effect that really
makes people doubt your integrity.

Freeze Frame and Slo Mo

These are breakdancing-type moves that apply to surfing
and rapid running. The Freeze Frame is done when you are
assured of a long, stable period. Simply freeze your motion
for as long as possible. Done correctly, a viewer's attention
will go from you to the river and back to you again, as you
go back into motion. This is especially good for surfing. Slo
Mo is, as the name implies, paddling in slow motion during
a surf or run. It is very difficult to maintain and requires

great anticipation. Try to enter an entirely new space and timing. This is a freaky move to watch and creates the illusion that the rider is very strange.

Boofing

This is a technique for running vertical drops with control. Perfected by the boaters on the Upper Yough, it was named by Phil Coleman in the mid-seventies.

Many people do this unawares, but squirt boaters are quite conscious of the finer points involved. Basically, you are doing a jump off the shoulder of a rock's pillow and landing flat in the eddy behind it. The hull makes a "boof" sound if it lands correctly; thus, the name. The strokes leading to a Boof should accelerate with the final one sinking the stern a bit, to ensure a flat charc over the drop. This is the highest control way of running pool drop-type drops. It keeps riders from floundering in the foam of deep, steep holes, contemplating their fate. On high Boofs, like waterfalls, I like to take an air stroke on the way down. This helps counter the energy from the last stroke and sets a low brace for the landing. If you don't need the brace, you're also set for a forward stroke, on the opposite side. It not only looks flashy, it makes the falls seem more like a rapid.

Be careful boofing very high waterfalls more than twenty feet, because, if you land in greenwater, the landing can be hard enough to hurt your back. In these cases, it may be best to let the bow dip under a little water as it lands, to cushion the fall and curve the charcs out.

ATTAINING

"Attaining" is the term I coined in the late 1970s for paddling upstream. This is quite a fine form of fun. There are even attaining races, which are great entertainment. If you want to perfect your attaining skills, for whatever reason, remember a few basic tips. Timing and accuracy are much more important here than in downstream negotiations: plan your lines well in advance and let the river dictate the timing; and pace your energy expenditure so you will have the fierce energy necessary for the tough attainments. Learn to feel the force surround you, and you will be able to attain up paper-thin eddies that are hundreds of feet long.

The basic techniques involve leaving eddies with maximum energy and charc. It is essential to leave the eddy as near to the rock as possible, using accelerating strokes into

the breakaway. This helps the boat hydroplane when it hits the downstream currents. Try to use a bowed charc that will sweep close to the rock. If you're leaving to the attainer's right side of the rock, the bow should start at the right side of the eddy on the downstream end, to the left side halfway to the rock, and veer back to exit within inches of the rock. You might use the downstream end of the eddy as a place to rest a stroke or two and fix your charc. Try to minimize your accelerating strokes on exit to three or four. Any more and you may peak out your hull speed too early or even generate bottom drag from the bottom of the river.

Peak out your hull only for brief periods of time, as it is a highly anaerobic activity. Try to alternate the aerobic and anaerobic work done by your muscles. The anaerobic work happens when you're under so much stress you can't breathe enough to supply your muscles with adequate oxygen. The muscles then burn extra carbohydrates, which leaves lactic acid as a calling card for the work done. It is important to "breathe" your muscles by slowing your pace to where your lungs are supplying enough oxygen and your circulation is floating all that nasty lactic acid out of your muscles. This lowers the amount of pain endured and lengthens the time you can spend working. In essence, use bursts of energy to attain positions where you can have bursts of rest. It also helps to hyperventilate a little just before a fierce attainment. This, of course, supercharges the muscles, letting you paddle at peak a little harder and longer. Be very conscious of bottom drag. Accelerating strokes pull you away from the bottom drag but can only accelerate for a limited amount of time. Think of your wake, its position and shape. You can attain to a shallow area and wait for your wake to catch you and then use its surf energy to support your progress. If you want to make a burst, wait until you are high on your wake and then burst

away, exploiting every quantum of surf energy. This technique minimizes the effects of bottom drag.

One's attention should be on charc, position, bursts, and freshness, in order of importance. You should be exhausted by the top of the rapid, so it doesn't really matter where you spend your energy, as long as you have the stuff required to push beyond the challenge created by each attainment along the way. Charc so that you soak up maximum eddy energy and leave the eddy on a burst that eventually climbs you up the pillow of the same rock. At the crest of the pillow, your upstream speed has stopped. It helps to pause at this point: the "position" (where you end up when your burst has played out). Then burst again to the next eddy; your position is what affords you rest. Your charc should keep the boat moving, no matter how slowly. You restart your charc at the position, at a point just upstream of the rock you just attained around.

Bursts should be used often, with their timing totally dictated by the river. Resting restores freshness and seems to come naturally when needed. However, a good attainer is used to going long and hard with his heart pounding out of his chest and enormous volumes of air howling through his tubes. The less time you spend on a single attainment, the less total energy you will use. The key is to match your bursts against the peak energies you will meet by accelerating into the encounter, to attain a new position. Freshness allows you to burst again from the new position and keeps you in control of your charc.

To attain small riffles, use micro-eddies hundreds of feet long. It also helps to use choppy, fast strokes, about 120 to140 per minute. If you need rest, let your wake catch you to help hold your position.

All in all, attaining is one of the most exciting aspects of the kayak world. Remember to wail like there's no tomorrow. Some attainments are nearly do-or-die events. Develop concentration, form, and timing. Maximize your impact on the currents you encounter with steep charcs. Absolutely push your limits till you're almost sick from exhaustion. This is good for you, though I'm not sure how. Never forget the "big three" they teach to raft guides: rock, water, and air. Use the water to avoid rocks and stay connected to air.

SURFING

"Surfing" is one of the more cosmic aspects of the sport. A joy for unskilled boaters, it is also a format for high skill. While

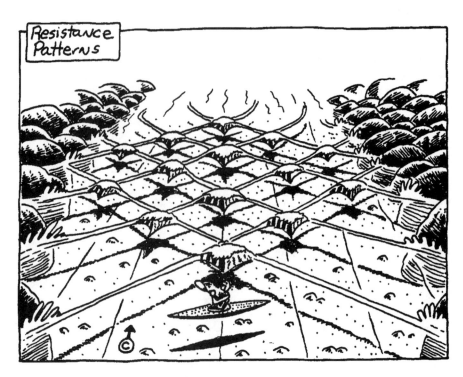

everyone has his special way of surfing, and doesn't really
need advice, a few hints can lead to longer, more controlled
surfs. Remember a clean, controlled exit is the only way to go.

There are two basic areas of focus while surfing. The first
is the static realm. This refers to the shape of the wave and
its neighboring eddies before you arrive. Surfable waves are
almost always caused by a fast section of water hitting a slow
area. The waves are a kind of rush hour pileup. To understand the wave's structure you have to understand the structure of the energies creating it. Think of the shape of the
greenwater slab just upstream of the wave. Then, think how
it is piling into the resistance generated by the neighboring
eddies, which lie to the side of and downstream of the wave.
Think of the shape of the resistance patterns, developed in
the form of sheer layers moving in alignment with the shape
of the riverbed. They're like multiple pillows built up from the
riverbed. The pillow effect diminishes towards the core of the
river but always remains aligned, and so, can be found. The
shape of the wave is aligned exactly with the merging of the
greenwater's charcs and the resistance.

In essence, surfing a wave is dancing on the interplay
between the two energies, motion and stillness. The arena is

a river-sized phenomenon scaled down to one wave. A good surf requires jockeying for position on the static energies in order to parry the energy from the dynamic energies. The dynamic energy is your power source for lateral progress, and so is used in a direct return system to deal with itself. The karmic implications are instant for the wave and the rider.

This brings up the second area of focus: the dynamic. The key concept of this realm naturally deals with change. There are two major generators of change here. The first is the fact that we perceive time in a linear fashion; that is, we believe one thing leads to another. This means that no matter how sweet or static a spot we find to ride, we will eventually charc away. We live in a dynamic realm and can't freeze a wave so it will treat us with consistency. In fact, quite the opposite occurs. Our presence loosens up a wave. Our boat creates a deep crease in the crest of the wave. Here is the second generator of change, the fact that our boat changes the shape and performance of the wave. This is a vicious cycle of change, which we participate in, sometimes unknowingly. Hull changes wave, which changes ride, which changes wave, and so on. Your wake while surfing can make the wave glass out or break. The effects generated by the hull are always secondary to the effects of the greenwater slab, and so try to focus on the slab more than the fireworks behind your back. After a while, you will notice how the wake effects are almost predictable. Wake effects are significant on thin waves. These are waves with minimal water shooting to the crest. They are usually glassy and rarely break. The crest is so thin you can only surf the base of the wave. Don't be afraid to pearl a bit; most boats won't ender until you tell them to. Even a couple of inches of water skimming over your deck won't appreciably alter your surf.

Most waves can be surfed on the crest or the base. Moving from a base surf to a crest surf requires several strong cutbacks to let the current lift your boat to the crest. Another alternative is to surf to the shoulder, and then up the shoulder to the crest. This seems more controlled but makes it easy to fall off the back of the wave. Crest-surfing demands much skill. The bow will stick straight out, cantilevered level out over the trough. Concentrate on the pull generated by the water falling down the back of the wave. Use the pull to keep the bow from being totally involved with the gravity of the trough. Use a lot of body English to maintain control by leaning hard, forward and back, and swooping into your cutbacks.

Flatspins are a performance phenomena brought on by rodeo boats. It infers doing a flat 360-degree spin (or several) while surfing any kind of wave, even a small green one. Flatspins require a flat-hulled boat with sharp chines. Each wave has different nuances which dictate the form of a Flatspin, but there are a few basics which apply to most scenarios. It's best to start your Flatspin when you are high on the wave. The spin can make you go lower on the wave as you go and you need a little wave face to use up. Try to synchronize with the natural rhythm of your surfing cutbacks. The backstroke needs to be accompanied by a leveling of the hull of the boat with the surface of the wave. You want the upstream edge lifted only the slightest amount to keep it from tipping. The idea is to use a single backstroke to fetch your first 180-degree spin. The next 180-degree spin is often the most difficult for people learning this technique. The foot area and bow of the boat tend to dig into the surface of the wave and generate too much friction. To counter this you can keep concentrating on keeping the hull flat to the surface of the wave and make sure your positioning on the wave has not gone askew. You don't want to be too low or off to the side of the sweetest section of the wave. If you are, pause for a moment and regain good position before trying. Because of this aspect, your second stroke—to establish your backsurf—is a good point to focus on. It can take any form, but the idea is to hone in on a good position on the wave before cranking the final 180 degrees to reestablish your front surf. With the right kind of flat-hulled boat (round-hulled boats are nearly impossible to flatspin) you can usually flatspin ad nauseum on a good wave. Often squirt boats are so dense that they sit deeper in a wave than a rodeo boat would and are harder to release and get to skip on the surface. You can help counter this aspect by using cutbacks to keep the boat loose and planing. You can feel when the hull has loosened up enough to flatspin while you are surfing. When it hits a certain speed of interaction, it enters a whole new valence of looseness. The thing to remember is that you can lose this looseness if you pause or dig into the wave. So keep it moving.

Try to do justice to the wave and reflect its finer qualities. Remember that you are riding only moments framed in the eternity of the wave's existence. You are riding an entity that has existed for millennia and yet is new every instant. It beats our act on all counts. Feel the resistance. Feel the currents from upstream. Feel the changes you make in the wave. And above all, feel great.

RUNNING RAPIDS IN SQUIRT BOATS

As a truly unique whitewater craft, a squirt boat requires some unique rapid-running techniques. Although it may not be obvious to the uninitiated, squirt boats create opportunities that far outweigh their handicaps. A good strategy includes provisions for both. While big-water rapids are different from highly technical ones, some concepts apply in both arenas. Strategy and skill must come into play in order to compensate for the lack of buoyancy. Expert squirtists try to align perfectly with the shreds of current which will play out into a royal ride. It all revolves around running what you read and reading clean lines. Beginners often find themselves experimenting with lines that they don't know well. This is a poor learning format because the success or failure of the encounter is beyond their control. It is just as wrong to take credit for the possible success as it is to get hammered for the possible failure. Charc in

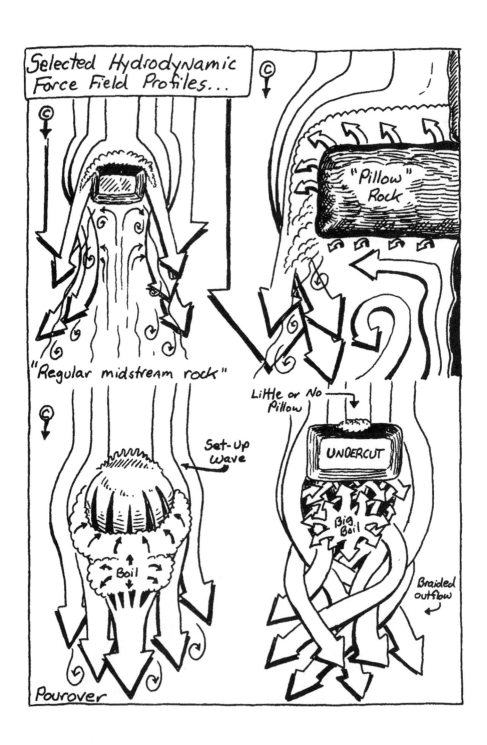

178

equals charc out. A lack of intent will always become apparent.

Technical rapids and big water both have pillows formed by rocks in the current. The "boofs" often used by boaters in technical water demand charcs that pierce these pillows. In big water, squirt boaters can boof pillows by bouncing their hulls off them similar to the way a downhill skier boofs moguls. You need to control the degree at which you pierce into and then roll off the pillows. Boofing pillows is a stretched-out version of splat charcs because you are dancing on the interface between the pillows and the downstream currents. The boat does not have to be vertical or get near the rock, however. The key to success here is establishing a lateral or diagonal momentum in order to minimize the degree at which your hull pierces the pillow. The concept is similar to the principle behind leaning a motorcycle through a turn. The lateral charcs can be established from previous pillow boofs, diagonal charcs set in wave trains, or from any other point where the boat sits flat on consistent currents.

There are many advantages to using pillow boofs. Pillows are very readable and constitute some of the more stable features in heavy currents; they can be used to slow down the action in Class V whitewater. The brief pause can be used to scout what lies beyond and set new charcs. Pillows are also the gateway to safe lines which lie between the exploding crests of huge waves and the surging whirlpools of eddy lines. Pillow boofs may not work on rocks with undercut corners because the poorly formed pillows may precipitate contact with the rock.

This is why it is advisable to boof a good distance from any rock, near where the pillow is just forming. Concentrate on perfecting your lateral momentum and leaning slightly to the back and inside of the turn. Try to avoid stalling parallel to the pillow unless you have set a good exit charc for the Mystery Move that can occur. It is best to pierce all the approach waters to a point where the pillow is cleanly pouring around the corner of the rock, connect to these, and reestablish control on your way around the corner.

Diagonal charcs are probably the most significant factor in a high-control format for squirt boats. A diagonal charc can quickly turn into an upstream ferry charc if you need to go to shore or wait for any reason. The technique applies to pillow boofs, running huge waves, avoiding pourovers, and a wide array of hot-dog maneuvers. The problem with running through the heart of huge waves is that they tend to

Moguling Moguls

Boofing Pillows

have one shoulder or another dominate the action at any one time. This results in what boaters refer to as "exploding" waves. If you are running unfamiliar waters, it is best to avoid being reduced to shrapnel status. Diagonal charcs are a means for establishing control in this arena. One of the few areas of consistent proportions in heavy waters is the base of large waves. One charc that works here is to cross the base and break through the shoulder about halfway up to the crest. Even if the crest explodes on your stern you can stay in control. Another workable charc is to run on one side of the crests of a wave train. This affords maximum visibility because it minimizes the splash and raises your boat to a height for scouting. If you are in known safe waters you should feel free to rocket move from the exploding crest of big waves. If your timing is right you can explode with the crest and attain a birdlike awareness. This kind of maneuver is both photogenic and memorable.

Remember you can always read bad pourovers by their steam and their "setup" wave. The set-up wave is a thin high wave formed just over the rock that makes the pourover. These waves are different from others because they are not part of a consistent wave train and lack follow-up waves. The axiom "If you can't see it, don't run it" applies here. Pourovers always have a distinct pillowlike current that can act like a force field upstream of them. These currents can be used to avoid the hole if you use them right. They can help you if you are in an upstream ferry mode. As a last-ditch effort, you could conceivably surf the setup wave to safety. To fall into a pourover type hole means you have pierced its pillows, ignoring their hints to turn away. Try to stay receptive to these hints as you run and you can enhance your longevity. This is a technique you can develop by running familiar rivers at night with no moon (running with a full moon is really pretty wimpy, isn't it?). When you are expert at this means of navigation you will know that insight is 20/20.

Entrapments are the number one menace to squirt boaters. It is a good idea to avoid rocks near shore on high-water runs because these rocks are often undercut and have weak pillows. It is also smart to boof any drop that is near vertical to avoid "pitoning" into rocks that may be hiding in the foam. Pitoning is very painful and dangerous— quite possibly lethal.

Keeping the boat flat in unfamiliar waters will improve your response time. If you ever pin broadside on one or two rocks you should try to re-level the boat and then push around the side. This can be accomplished by skulling braces or jamming your paddle to the floor of the river. Squirt boats are so thin they can usually carve their way back to level. Another option on a good single-rock pin is to spin the boat vertically to Splat mode and then go around the rock's corner. You also have the effects of the offending rock's pillow to help calm the neighboring waters. If you find you can't re-level and one or two good shakes don't free you up, be sure to spend little time deciding to exit your boat. Most squirt boats hold up very well to compression and won't collapse.

With all the good ideas to adhere to, it may seem as though getting down the river is a major accomplishment in a squirt boat. It is. But there are a lot of extra, fun things to do as we fall into the persuasion of gravity. Expert squirtists have tremendous abdominal muscles due to the endless pursuit of fun. Somewhere there is a magic incentive that makes squirtists strive to flow like the river. No one will ever be able to put a name on it; whatever it is, you take it to the grave with you.

SQUIRTIPS

Squirt boating is a dynamic, athletic art form, lending itself to creativity and exertion. It has an inherent discipline which has a powerful incentive—a good ride. Energy efficiency is the basis of good form. To attain cubic ability, the mentality must precede the reality. You must be curious about what lies beyond the envelope of your ability and you must have an appetite for it. Then the challenge is to mount a strategic, centered attempt. An initial energy is established and then coached through a move. This energy is focused in the leading edge of the boat. What we do with our balance and paddle adds or detracts from the integrity of that energy. The energy is there to use, lose, or confuse. The thing to keep in mind is that the learning curve is endless and so we must enjoy the learning process itself. With these as givens I've come up with some observations about one's participation in this sport.

The strategy of squirt boating has two formats: what and where. Squirt moves can be done almost anywhere and so this is a huge subject undergoing constant change. You could divide the "wheres" into familiar or unfamiliar arenas and attach levels of caution to each, but I prefer to consider each attempt as a new learning experience that could kill me. So I try to stay on my toes. For squirt boating—using deep, three-dimensional features of the current—it helps to have a cubic view of the river. The thing to realize is that the current, and your participation with it, is more a function of shape than of power. You must fit the shapes of the water features to find the path of least resistance. I see the river as a central core of current molded into a certain path. It is buffed into shape by pillows on rocks. This means every rock on the bottom of the river adds to the shape of the pillow structures there. Think of it as layers of resistance built infinitely towards the river's core. The river's core tends to splay dendritically to feed these pillows but without losing its main trunk of energy. A quality squirt move will align itself with these layers of energy/resistance and actually display their existence. In other words, the style has to fit right if it's going to look good.

The "whats" generally include new or established moves. As a person tries to assemble a move, I see them as passing through three learning stages. The first stage can be thought of as *focus*. A person will be enticed into a move by remembering an aspect of the charc but without being real clear on the particulars. As they try to assemble the move they will run into bumpy parts of the move, usually just before the exit brace. The way to correction is through the entrance charc, but first the person must make a critical leap of commitment to initially grasp the feelings and positioning of the move. Once the path of energy and braces has been established, it's easier to go back and clean up the tricky parts. After you have initially broken through to the exit brace of a move, I recommend you try a learning series of low energy attempts to feel out the move and find the points where you can regain control. This is usually at stations where the volume of the boat is trapped directly below you and you can free your stick and stretch into the next section of the move. The second stage of move acquisition is marked by *fluidity*. At this point most people feel they have mastered the move, but they have one persistent problem—their fellow boaters. The little charc bumps our buddies inadvertently give us are just enough to skew our charcs and keep us from attaining a good energy flow into the move. The way to deal with this predicament is by doing what I call "defending the staging area." The staging area is the last place you can comfortably set a good charc into a move. You can defend the area by talking to intruders and explaining your space, pushing boats away with your hand, or simply extending the pointy ends of your equipment towards the intruder and leaving the onus on them to deal with it. Once the staging area has been successfully defended, and the way is clear into the move, go for it with a clear conscience and a clean charc and enjoy. This stage is a hang-up for many people because they can't get over the fellow charcist problem. The way to deal with it is to keep in mind that your participation with these people has an effect on them. Mold the effect to your liking but try to keep in mind what kind of vibe you appreciate from a crew—some combination of solid *and* fun. If you want people to respect your space, simply respect theirs while insisting on the quality of your charc. It is also key to remember that your move is really an effect on the others of your trip, not just an *effect* on your boat, paddle, and the river. The observer of a move can, and will, affect its outcome just by being part of the arena.

The third learning stage is, of course, what I would consider a peak learning level. It is the move in full force use in a timely bid for fun. It is noticeably different from a practice move because it is unpremeditated and uninhibited. It's hard to describe but it can be thought of as *dynamic*. You can tell you're there when the river seems to fit the ride and vice versa. It is actual working fun and I refer to it as "serendipitous behavior" or "serendiposity." It's kind of like being lucky and good at the same time. There are two things to keep in mind at this stage. The first is that *any move is a series of feelings*. You feel your way in to secure your way out. There is a flow of energy related to the move and its efficiency is a matter of discipline. Bad form degrades your energy, good form restores it. The second thing to bear in mind is that this is a learning stage. You are learning the shape of the river. Your boat has become a creative exploring tool.

The bottom line is that you are a wing of specific density with a set of abs as a transmission and a set of arms as grabbers/tweakers. Efficiency demands that you maintain minimal turbulent flow across your deck. This is maintained through a minimal angle of attack of the wing. You will have a specific initial energy to sink a specific volume to a specific depth. Success is dependent on your bid for verticality being backed by your efficiency in harvesting energy. Maintaining clean basic form allows energy to feed through the move easier, which allows for more control at critical junctures. It becomes a matter of cleaning your stations for the tougher moves. For Mystery Moves it's a science of wings into slabs and underwater orientation. I actually think a lot of squirt development is dependent on abdominal muscle development. You have to grow tuned abs, the science of "abdology." You also need to develop skills to hunt the path of least resistance for any move—be lazy, but alert. Things can be low-key but high energy, high control but on the fringe of your abilities.

We are talking about access to fun and high performance. A way of peaking one's abilities. A peaked paddler will have a unique style as per their body type and mentality. Enjoy your uniqueness but realize that clean form is marked by a feeling of carried-over and molded energy—handled energy. Let the boat do the bulk of the work and use your muscles to guide the energy stored in the leading edge of the boat. Remember a move is a *series of feelings* and squirt boating is a way of feeling a river. In a squirt boat you are deeply involved in hydrodynamics to such a degree that you should probably be committed. It's cool to be at one with the currents, but only if it's the right currents. Develop the power of your charc by respecting the shape of the river, the shape of the move, and the shape of the crew. You must focus all of your energy in the leading edge and use the boat as a tool. You must dominate the boat while submitting to the river. You must tune to the shape of the river while persistently focusing the boat's energy. Tough moves require unbending intent.

It sounds tough. But the fact is that it is merely a gauntlet of distractions. Ignore the distractions and keep your eyes on the prize and you'll make good progress. Don't exhaust yourself. Do it for fun. If you find yourself tight or tense just think of a cat. You want your fur loose like a cat in a fight. You want instant reactions. You want the ride.

FUTURE FUN

Where do squirt boats belong in the future? Can we get a sense of direction from the past or are we on the brink of being found—after having once "been lost"? Or is "being lost" the worthy endgame of true Mystery obsessions? It's encouraging that so many people are daring to design squirt boats now. It represents people shaping their tools for the best compromise between their desires and their environment. It's part of the tweaking process.

Presently at the core of this evolution is an interesting conflict. It's the debate between flatspinnability and Mystery Move friendliness. Flatspins require an abrupt "trailing edge" to the hull's surface, in any direction, to shunt currents off the hull efficiently so they have minimal drag. This bestows coveted "looseness" on the hull. Unfortunately this is the same edge which functions as a "leading edge" to the cross section of the boat as it works as a wing underwater during Mystery Moves. An abrupt corner on a leading edge of a wing separates the boundary layer and generates drag. This drag registers as a stripping away of forward energy during the Mystery, leading to a propensity to stall. There is certainly a middle ground to the debate and it is now being explored. At issue are the width of the boat, the handling of the ends of the boat, the volume and the boxiness of the central section of the boat, and how tucked away the flatspin-required corners are.

A wider boat with wider end shapes spins in a plane easier and flatspins better but is more of a "speed wing" (thin and long with minimal drag at low angles of attack) than an "acrobatic wing" (fat and short, but slow, with low drag at high angles of attack). This means it has to "carve" turns around its long axis in Screw mode—as opposed to mushing or spinning its way around the true center of the boat. The large planar sections of hull required for flatspins also tend to coax the hull's activity into a planar orientation. A rounded hull and leading edge allows infinite tweaking and jostling during screws because the flat isn't bossing the action. This translates to adaptability in turbulent arenas. The flats and corners of a flatspin hull also serve to register "chatter" from the many currents hitting the boat at any one moment. They act as a sounding board for these currents to bounce off of, and these vibrations render a wiggly feel in chaotic waters such as when running a Class IV rapid or setting up for a Mystery in squirrely waters. A rounder hull tends to mush into whatever currents encroach on it and buffer them. Lacking corners, it has fewer ways for the currents to apply leverage.

Having the central area of the boat be boxy and big helps it stay aloof for flatspins but completely works against what's needed for big roaming mysteries—density and a soft feel. A sharp trailing edge at the outermost point of the hull makes for the best flatspinning, but having this edge chamfered back a bit creates a leading edge which works at a higher variety of angles of attack. This is an aspect where a lot of development will have to happen.

Key to this issue is the amount of time and number of arenas where squirt boaters sink or surf. Some squirtists want a do-everything boat and they need a flatspinnable hull to fully exploit their favored sections of river. Others are pure downtime seekers who just want a boat that cruises nicely, surfs some, and sinks with abandon. Squirtists nowadays can focus their equipment on the nature of ride they prefer. So the shape of the future of the sport will embody the passions of the riders.

The purist downtime artists often shun or ignore flatwater disciplines. Indeed, cartwheeling in a Mystery circle (a procession of squirt boaters at a single Mystery arena) is a sure sign of a rookie. Why? Because Cartwheels use up precious "foot time" (the amount of time you can endure in a squirt boat before your feet really hurt) and significantly increase the stress on your feet. They also can endanger and distract others in the line and make you alter your timing and positioning on your way to the next Mystery. Cartwheels in Mystery circles seem to say, "I don't get this Mystery stuff, but just watch me shred my ends!" Mystery seekers seldom even notice this boorish activity, let alone respect it.

On the contrary, flatwater skills, like the Test, are a test of abs and control and a celebration of the cubic freedom encompassed in the sport. The Japanese squirt artists are pure squirtists and they can make flatwater work look like art. Compared to rodeo boats, flatwater squirting is effortless grace. And the high energy dynamics of flatspins and surf flight is anything but boring. There is a "Golden Fleece" sought of a true "total" design. I think it's a myth, but its pursuit is probably worthwhile, in spite of the fact that its resolution will always be necessarily postured as a kind of compromise.

There is another future pursuit of squirt designers—down-time machines. When designers turn their talents to extend-ing downtime, present limits (in the neighborhood of thirty seconds) will be crushed. Unlimited downtime is within grasp. It's a function of density and shape and there are a huge number of variations of such yet to be sampled. It leaves the future of the sport in question. If the downtime purists gain total ability, where will their horizon lie? Even the great beyond has a limit to mere humans. Appetite will be satiated. This is a very dangerous consideration for depth chargers. To lose your curiosity of the deep is a formidable concern. It will affect your Mystery performance. Even with air tanks and safe arenas, the charm could wear off with limitless ability. And designers will be able to provide limit-less ability when they turn their attention to this facet.

No Mystery artist can forsake the lure of the deep. But is it the "future"? Record after record will fall, but is the point of the sport to endure underwater? There are so many va-garies to roaming underwater, one can wonder, "What *is* the point?". This is where the Mystery Trance has its influence. After a long Mystery session you become a Mystery zombie and gain a sort of tunnel vision. You can become so one with your charc that you are spiritually consumed by it. I am naturally suspicious of this condition and wonder if it is pure. I feel the Mystery Trance detracts from your ability in the realm. It can slow your reaction to a sudden disaster, like an unexpected pinning situation. These things do happen. So, the deep is fraught with vagaries and to roam the deep is to navigate the vagaries. What are the performance criteria? What is good and what is less? What is really meaningful?

I see another future for squirt pursuits. Total cubic ability is best achieved underwater. Without the water's surface to ref-erence and smash through, and with subsurface currents charging the action, underwater maneuvering is a potent realm for exploration. Loops are just one aspect of this. Multiple Loops and underwater Cartwheels are more what I have in mind. And there is a lot of mapping and awareness which applies to this aspect. Consider that one of the great detriments to big downtime is getting lost. Underwater map-ping—both in timing and space—is an unfolding science and the antithesis of the Trance. Consider recent exploits of Trip Kenny, the Tall One and a DT virtuoso. He consciously finds his way around the depths of Cowbell (a favored arena on the Nolichucky River) to such a degree that he catches eddies underwater, goes back upstream and turns out again, all subsurface. This "knowing your way around" is passed on squirtist to squirtist and has become a valuable body of knowledge in the sport. Knowledge of local Mystery dangers is passed on this way.

This evolution of mapping and technique mirrors another significant personal growth brought on by Mystery experiences. Simply put, it involves staying cool underwater. True Mystery hogs are cool beyond conception in deep, dark, and violent realms. Beginners get skittish with even shallow Mysteries. After all, you are deliberately putting your head underwater and traveling to unseen depths. To crush into a pin deep in a Mystery can be a life-altering event and one not soon forgotten. Being nervous is not stupid, but it does give you a hair trigger "up button" (even the slightest urge to reemerge will send you skyward). How did the experts get so cool in the deep? Mapping and technique. Appetite and tenacity.

Maybe a path for the sport lies in these touchstones. The sport is very informal and independent. This makes it robust and flexible. These principals do point a way for future charcs. I think there is a lot of room to move with "sweet" charcs. How sweet can a charc be? How earnest and pure? As sweet as air after an unsettling Mystery? As sweet as clean waters, bright sun, and sparkly serendiposity? I tell

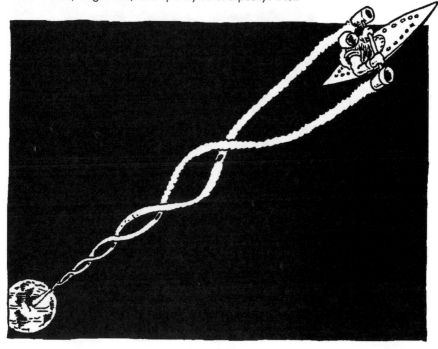

Leaning back on a powerful stroke at the lip of the falls ensures a Boof landing.

you sweetness is unlimited but personal. At least it **can** be known. So pursue it doggedly. This doesn't mean the river won't betray your sweet ambitions and martyr you, vanishing you from the face of the earth forever in a moment. But it does mean you can reach the highest highs of amphibiosity and "mer"ciful grace. You can't guarantee your safety, and you can't fully succumb to the Trance, but you can fly and blend, if only for moments. And the shape of the ride will shape your soul. Your intent will become manifest. What shape will all this take? I would say it's a question . . . of style. I trust it will be a sweet style. I know it will be filled with all the implications of a soberingly intoxicating world of bubbles—the Champagne World. Remember the **real** squirt realm is one of **feel**. This is all you need to know. Feeling after feeling, time after time, you must trust yourself to unleash your perspective on the awesome. Are you ready for this kind of ride? I think so.

SELECTED
INTERVIEWS

I have taken the opportunity to interview significant players in the development of squirt sport in America. Each interview gives insight into the thinkings and personalities of these paddlers. They are also full of interesting historical facts and relevant tips for perfecting techniques. I hope you enjoy their answers as much as I do.

INTERVIEW WITH JESSE WHITTEMORE

JIM: You are considered the true grandfather of squirt boating because you did the first Backender squirts. Everyone thought you were being dangerous. Did it seem dangerous to you?

JESSE: Danger didn't enter the picture until splattering and pillow moves. Proven by Jeff S. one day on the Big Sandy in the early 1980s [see "Early History" in the Introduction]. It seemed like the beginning of something everyone would want to do. At the time, Enders were all the craze to the masses, so being able to ender anywhere naturally would take the attention and desire of the many. All these thoughts of detonating an explosion did enter my mind, but the ever-present foundation of my philosophy and love was to endeavor to be able to read the invisible currents of whitewater on a three-dimensional level through Clues found on the surface, to be a better boater, to dissolve the squirrels and mysteries, to be in *balance* and *efficient* wherever you are. The trick was to *see* what you could not. Squirt boating and all its moves in all the different places on the river were merely the fun side effect of my need to learn. Squirting is the act of learning whitewater on the 3-D level to me. Nothing more. Some fame, women, and glory were also way up there with the feel of splattering Pillow Rock.

JIM: You also pioneered the first run of Big Splat rapid on the Big Sandy River in West Virginia—in a squirt boat no less. Can you describe what it was like to do that? What was your first run like and when was it?

JESSE: A 13'2" flat no-rocker boat was to me the art at the time. I could have it all—submersion boating, big time slots and eddies, attaining drops with the best of them, and waterfalls. Big Splat simply looked runnable one day. I ran it three times that day. I can remember being on such an ego high. Then, in front of half a dozen friends at First Island on the first drop, I pinned vertically and, while climbing out, the river stripped me of my dignity and shorts in front of friends and God. Big Splat was scary, very scary. My success built on my river-reading confidence.

JIM: You were also one of the first kayakers to ever

go on "tour" for a manufacturer when you helped Perception market the Sabre. This gave many, many people their first glimpse of squirt boating. When was this and what kind of reactions did you get from people when they saw you blasting into the third dimension?

JESSE: Perception sent me down South, up North, out West, and to Europe. I very much appreciate their support and enthusiasm for me and the sport of whitewater. This all took place between 1984 and 1985. When I went out west, the thing to do was twirl your paddle while sitting sideways in the hole. At the Payette River rodeo that is all they did. I blast-surfed stern and bow, wave moved, cart-wheeled, and a couple of other things that someone probably has names for. I thought, "Use that paddle!" and showed them how. They are using their paddles now. Reaction was mixed. Some had splendid wonder and excitement. Others may have been overwhelmed how far behind they were. Another instant was splattering con-crete rocks on the Augsburg, Germany, slalom course at the end of the race in front of thousands of people. The worse I got trashed, the louder the roar of the people. I even heard them underwater. That was cool.

JIM: Your custom kayak graphics are still consid-ered artwork. Did you do most of them from cus-tomer requests or did you have a free hand to create them as you pleased?

JESSE: When people asked for specific artwork, the love was lost and it did not turn out as well as if someone said, "Go for it." I particularly went extra for people I liked or wanted to know better. I love creative art time. I felt fortunate to have a medium where I could express myself and make a living.

JIM: I remember you used to be quite a sight with your huge Slasher paddle, sparkly boat, and Darth Vader helmet on the Upper Gauley. I remember you blowing away crowds with daring and dynamic Blasts. Do you ever get the urge to go do that again, just because you *can*?

JESSE: I still do it to a different extent. The world of boat-ing's eyes are on rodeo/squirt boating. Nothing else exists to the masses. And why would you want to anyway? Well, my most favored corner of the sport is slalom-style kayaking. A lot of times I get stares from these new-schoolers who obviously have never seen a slalom boat, much less what they can do. I have been training very hard this year and I can make their eyes open, especially at Attaining. I still got it, it's just changed.

JIM: You are a key person at Mountain Surf now. What do you do for them?

JESSE: I am their operations manager, co-designer, and R&D man. I keep the quality standard where John Mason wants it, problem solve on all levels, and catch the releases every time, bless their heart.

JIM: You are in the best shape of your twenty-plus year paddling career and a contender in any race you enter. How often do you paddle?

JESSE: I'm 42. I get up every morning at 5 a.m., do 400 push-ups and 400 sit-ups with a 10-pound weight behind my head. I go to work at 7:30 a.m., get off, catch the dam release if there is one and, if not, I go to the Loop for at least a one hour work-out. Frequently each week, I wear a heart rate monitor and keep my heart rate up to170-plus for at least 30 minutes. It's hard to do any-thing else except eat and sleep. I tell people I'm real busy and they think, "work." It's not. It's the love for my sport, getting the girl, and kicking new-schooler ass big time when they enter my arena.

JIM: Did your feet hurt way back then? Did you know it would be an issue forever for squirt boaters?

JESSE: Yes, it was apparent that if you wanted to drive the bow under with reasonable ease, your feet would suffer. I spent so much time in my boat that I got used to it. The formula seems to be "No pain, no gain."

JIM: No one has ever had your flair. Many paddlers now days seem to have no style and are just going through the motions. What's with that?

JESSE: Jim, you called it "blending." John Lugbill simply wouldn't proceed without one hundred percent intention of perfection in all of his movements. I believe that your time on the river is so valuable that putting nothing less than *all* your spirit in your movements and intentions is the only discipline for the purist. What people see may be the result of my intentions. I don't know. I haven't seen myself on a recording.

JIM: Squirt boating is entering its third decade and many argue that squirt performance standards inspired the rodeo craze. What's it like to be the guy who kick started it all?

JESSE: Squirting, Rodeo, and Playboating are all the same—the discovery and practice of understanding the three-dimensional shape of whitewater. Not many people know that I brought it into human perspective. I believe if it was not me, someone else would have put it together. I feel fortunate to have discovered something that so many people love so much and always will for as long as there will be rivers and people. It's huge for someone as small as me.

JIM: What advice can you give to beginning squirt boaters?

JESSE: My advice is realize your capabilities. Natural selection lives stronger nowhere else. When you think incorrectly, the consequences vary from missing knuckles to gone. There is a fine line of safety to dance. The wave warrior will choose the one of life and tolerable suffering.

INTERVIEW WITH JEFF SNYDER

JIM: You were one of the original pioneers of squirt boating. You are noted for bold hole play and Mystery Moves. What does "bold" mean to you?

JEFF: We usually use "bold" in context with something we would be uncomfortable with. So basically it's just a word usually aimed by those who just don't know. Another definition I have of bold is that "Bold is talking about something as if we know anything." Another definition is "Signing up for anything we are not ready for." "Bold" could and should stand for using lots of experience. It could be "Bodacious, Outrageous, Ludicrous, and Daring" or "Be On Line Darn it" or "Balance On Line Delicately."

JIM: You rarely lose your cool in intense situations. What does it take to improvise the way you do?

JEFF: Adrenaline and practice. I have said "Oh s***" sometimes, so I might get more credit than I've earned. After you scrap "Plan A" you just deal with whatever is going on.

JIM: You were one of the first paddlers to improvise cubic rodeo scenarios in monster holes in a squirt boat in the mid-eighties. Just what did you think you were doing?

JEFF: We were just experimentin' with centrifugal force, lethal power, and a whole lotta water.

JIM: Your style in a squirt boat is sweet but direct. What do you strive for in your charc?

JEFF: To build on what I know, mainly to stay safe and be lucky.

JIM: You've suffered some of the worst survivable accidents in squirt history. Are there any lessons you can share from this?

JEFF: There are very talented doctors nowadays. It's not much fun testing their skills. Always carry a plan (one way or the other).

JIM: After a rash of terrible deaths in the late nineties, I once asked you if you thought people should back off on their glorious ambitions. You said that wouldn't keep people from being hurt. What can people do to keep their act together?

JEFF: Pay attention to the signs nature offers. Stay organized, clean, and understanding. Know when to say uncle.

JIM: You've had a number of near death experiences in your long career and yet you don't dwell on those. What's it like to be so close to death, even for a moment?

JEFF: Near death experiences are nearly life-changing. What it has brought me to realize is how out of control we are as humans, and I think that leads to a peaceful feeling.

JIM: You are also responsible for turning many people on to higher levels of boating. What do you feel holds many people back from finding their true potential?

JEFF: Commitment, time, and money, but mostly the mind. If you doubt you can, you can't. Or if you think you can, you can!

JIM: So many people boat for varied and personal reasons. Why do you boat?

JEFF: Of course the original attraction is fame and fortune, but like others [I do it]for many reasons. Mostly it's instinct that I boat. I like most of the people and places it brings me to. It's a chance to showcase my abilities, to capture some attention, and influence friends toward knowledge and truth. My real reason is to learn, and it brings that feelin' money can't buy.

JIM: When you are seeking a truly epic Mystery, what do you concentrate on? Is there strategy involved, or pure willpower?

JEFF: Timing, hitting the door when it's open, and breathing. Then adjust to the submerging you were just asking for.

JIM: You are a pioneer of Striding, which is simply running whitewater standing up with a very long paddle. What's it like to run a big waterfall that way? What would a novice have to watch out for?

JEFF: It's like a magic carpet ride. Wait till the lip to fall and bend at the knees.

JIM: You can roll your boat standing up, which everyone knows is impossible. How can you dare to do the impossible?

JEFF: Impossible isn't improbable. What you say folks "know" is wrong, it's only improbable. I don't think of it as daring but existing.

JIM: What advice would you give someone who wants to experience the magic of the river?

JEFF: Plan ahead, be careful, and hide your tracks.

JIM: What makes a joyful river day for you?

JEFF: A night of snow or rain.

INTERVIEW WITH ERIC LINDBERG

JIM: When did you start squirt boating and what was your first squirt boat?

ERIC: Not sure about the exact year here. I got one of your Jet kits, so that puts it at 1985? I had managed to get in Whitney's Wide Ride and it was painful but fun. You were on to the Jet, so that's where I got to.

JIM: What was your "other" boat at the time?

ERIC: I had a glass Noah Jeti, short and round, plus a Seda surf ski that I got around 1980—wide, flat bottom, chines, and hard rails (sort of like all these "new" rodeo boat designs of the past few years).

JIM: What was it about squirt boats that appealed to you in those days?

ERIC: They were a total departure. I remember sitting on the rocks at the bottom of Tumblehome [Gauley River] after a long Ender session and seeing Jess Whittemore come through, get vertical, spin, work his way up the eddy, blast the hole at the bottom of Mailbox, squirt out of the eddy and head downstream. It took less than twenty seconds to watch, but I don't think I ever recovered. That's when I found the Ruth Bell Toy Company [the name of Jim's original company] and "Sparkaholics Anonymous." The real fun came in the river running. Squirt boats gave you such great access to the flow of the river, finding the thin green line in all the white, and the connection to *everything* that was going on, not just the surface. Then on a trip on the New at about four to six feet, while everyone was on the rocks eating, I was working an eddy line and got sucked into a fold. I didn't know then that squirt boats all come with an up button, so I stayed down long enough for everyone to get excited— the classic "Where's Eric? Where's Eric ...?" After that, I simply wanted more. Seeking downtime and finding the access was the focus. Wave moves had such a great feel, deep and high-speed heading downstream.

JIM: You were one of the squirt pioneers who found and named many of the classic squirt playspots on the Potomac. Which boat did a lot of this exploring happen in?

ERIC: First the Jet and then the ProJet. They were great boats.

JIM: A lot of what you explored were Mystery spots like the "Bermuda Triangle." What kind of down-times were you getting and do you feel as if you were maxing these spots out, or just learning about them?

ERIC: I never really tried to max Bermuda. There was always some uncertainty about whether you were heading upstream or down. Upstream was cool, down was nervous. I would have to guess at five to ten seconds, but I really don't remember. There were some sessions at Simple Pleasures, working the Mush Move access, that got consistent ten-plus [second] DT, with some longer.

JIM: With the loss of a couple close friends in 1989, Whitney Shields and Charlie Deaton, and old-school-ers at the time bemoaning the dangers of these "radically" low volume boats, you had to face in a very real way the hazards of squirt boating. What did you learn from this era and what made you persist?

ERIC: 1989 was definitely a hard year. We had come off of a couple of incredible seasons on the Gauley where we found Sweet Cheeks, Twisted Sister, and Sherlock. We were tagging lots of rocks, but even then others were pushing the lower limits. Woody and Risa were taking Jet boats down the Russell Fork and I remember a trip on Dougherty with Jeff in a low Jet boat. I was in my big old fat Jeti. So we felt like we were on the reasonable end of the spectrum. What I learned was the need to control your appetite so that you can still be hungry when you are pushing 100. And friends make even a taste into a banquet.

JIM: Whitney and yourself had epic pins deep in Mystery mode back then. Could you describe your experience?

ERIC: Both were eye-opening. Whitney's was one of those winter days below Great Falls at about eight feet. We had attained up and were on the Virginia side at a point below Fisherman's Eddy. [There were] wild boiling eddies with big surges. Whitney and I had just talked about the spot and recalled tagging rocks on the way out before. Whitney peeled out ahead of me and instantly

Mysteried, then stayed gone. Totally helpless at that point, the event lasted way too long, and he was nearly puking when he surfaced. I was playing a spot at the top of the back channel at something over six feet (attainer's left below a set of small waves with a small pourover feature). I had had good sessions there many times, shoulder to helmet with great Black Attacks. On this try, I decided to move out about 12 inches to get a little more DT. I instantly dropped and pinned—probably at least two feet under—broadside with the rock under my right thigh. Fortunately, I shook loose before the boat crushed. The pin was bad enough to break the skin and bruise my leg. Both events were ones of inches. Know the spots. Know all the features and probe. And still be cautious.

JIM: What would be an optimal squirt format for you to enjoy?

ERIC: This is easy. The past few years a few of us have been getting together for serious DT sessions. I have a few world-class Mystery spots near home. Day-long sessions with a few friends is hard to beat. My real focus is on quality, not adrenaline. Well, at least moderate the adrenaline. You have to have *some*. But controlled bottom time—cruising underwater trying to consistently get ten-plus seconds—is good.

JIM: You were the original developer of the Lindbergaskets which have become a popular Mountain Surf product because of their robust and superior seal. I remember you used a version for a couple years before anyone paid attention to the technology. What was it like to be ignored during this period?

ERIC: Pretty much a privilege. I was able to get in longer sessions without a line while everyone else was fooling with dumping their boat.

JIM: What advice would you give to a beginning squirtist?

ERIC: Learn to get chest deep in flatwater, stay safe, and Nose Korks are cool.

JIM: You are a "stealth boating" specialist. What is that?

ERIC: Not sure . . . I've heard rumors about folks getting epic sessions under ideal conditions with no crowd . . .

But you can't get any of them to give you details on how, when, or where.

JIM: You live exactly where you want to in central West Virginia. What kind of recreation do you have access to year-round?

ERIC: Lots more than I take advantage of. "Halls" ["of Karma"—New River] is 12 miles from the house, Upper G[auley] is 18 miles, "Twisted" ["Sister"- Gauley River] is a touch over an hour, mountain biking all around, and most winters some great snow boarding. Oh, and I live at the takeout for the upper Meadow.

INTERVIEW WITH JEFF SCHNELLE

JIM: You're well known as the Master of Downtime. Have you ever entered a contest?

JEFF: Yes. I did the Ocoee Rodeo years ago and had a blast, even though I never hit consistent Mysteries at that spot. I also entered the original Nolichucky Rodeo, where we squirted and did Mysteries at Cowbell then blasted at Jaws. It was a riot. I also had fun at the Potomac and New River Rodeos. The competition part is great, but the main enjoyment for me is just having fun with other squirters. We are a rare breed and getting twenty or thirty of us together to play doesn't happen very often.

JIM: Can you describe your one-of-a-kind boat?

JEFF: Certainly. It is a "Bigfoot Shred cut with a Groove Tube." You were perfecting your inflatable inner tube concept at that time and you had just completed a pumped up Shred deck mold for large people with the Groove Tube cockpit design. The hull is a Bigfoot hull, so I have comfy foot room with a minimal chop in a boat with a recessed cockpit. This cockpit minimizes turbulence and aids in control during long Mysteries.

JIM: You have done very many Mystery Moves longer than 20 seconds and travelling over 100 feet underwater. What techniques does this require? Do you go deep first and stay deep or slowly work deeper and deeper?

JEFF: The technique varies with the spot. The main advice I can give for long, deep Mysteries is to head the treading route [hand paddle]. With a stick, one blade or the other will be slowing your spin down and will shorten your downtime and send you up too soon. You can also only navigate with one blade at a time so your control is minimized. There are only a few people I have seen (you and Eric Lindberg) who have the Crossbow Duffek stroke down good enough to maximize your downtime with a stick. That technique doesn't work very well for me. With treading, you can use both hands simultaneously to help increase or decrease your spin speed to go up or down. If you want to go deeper and are spinning counterclockwise, sweep clockwise with your hands, alternating right then left to keep your balance. Your boat acts like a propeller to pull you down into the deeper currents. To attain to a higher elevation, slow down your spin and you will start ascending. I find that with a hand free to move on each side, it is easier to keep your balance, hence your weight, centered over your boat which keeps you from black attacking prematurely. That is the main problem I see people have when they are learning, keeping their weight centered over the boat. They black attack out of the move before they even get settled into a charc because of their uneven weight distribution.

JIM: Do you go to where it's dark and there's a lot of pressure on your epic Mystery Moves? Can you describe what it's like to return from such depths?

JEFF: Again, it depends on the spot. The most pressure I have felt is definitely at Halls of Karma. I used to Scuba dive and the pressure at Halls, to me, feels like the pressure I felt at 15 to 20 feet while diving. The hull of your boat is compressed against your legs, locking you in. Your spray skirt is sucked down between your legs, compressed against the bottom hull of your boat. It feels as if there is no escape and your only choice is to maintain your charc and ride it out until either the move plays out, or you run out of air and have to go into Emergency Black Attack Mode. To initiate a Skyrocket Black Attack from 18 feet deep while spinning counterclockwise, first lift up on your left knee to expose the left underside of your hull to the upward currents, then lean back and prepare for takeoff. I have had some exits where my head is thrown back on the stern because I shot to the surface so fast. Others, I might get in a Cartwheel or three on the way back to the top. Your exit charc varies with the currents around at that time so each ride back is unique. Just look up for rafts.

JIM: When you drop into long Mysteries at Twisted Sister on the Lower Gauley, you obviously have to navigate around a deep rock halfway through the Mystery which has pinned and hurt people. How do you do that?

JEFF: Ideally, there are two scenarios. The first is to slow down your spin and level out just above the rock. This is very hard to do and doesn't happen too often. If this works, you get pulled down after you pass the rock by the vortex of the current and are locked in for a great ride. I have been so locked in before that I have run out of air and black attacked back to the surface past the big rock at the bottom of the eddy on river left. This, to me, is the optimal Twisted Sister ride. The second scenario would be to tap into the instant downward charc and start bouncing along the bottom. It is cool because sometimes you are swirling in underwater whirlpools of leaves and debris and it is very violent down there. The current changes right before the rock, as you feel a slight uplift on your hull. If you shift your weight just right, you will bounce over the rock and continue on downstream after the vortex sucks you back down as you pass over the rock. This is the coolest ride but I have only accomplished this ten times or so. Some other not so optimal scenarios for me have been piton bow first into the rock, sit there for a second and get sucked around the side of the rock and shoot violently towards the surface; piton stern first, and end up like the above scenario, stick on the rock sideways and sit there, then push off with my hands (another benefit of treading) and shoot to the surface under uncontrollable charc; or bounce sideways off of the rock, regain charc, and continue for a long Mystery. There are always exciting rides in the Bad Neighborhood at the Sis.

JIM: Can you describe what it's like to hit the bottom of the river (15-plus feet deep) at the Halls of Karma Mystery arena on the New River?

JEFF: I have only accomplished this four times. Two of the times, my stern tapped the bottom as I initiated my Black Attack sequence. The other two times were wild. I treaded into a very tight and deep charc right next to the rock at the Halls. My angle of attack was very steep as I engaged the greenwater slab. It felt like an elevator as the bottom dropped out from under me and I got sucked straight down next to the big rock at the entrance. My spin speed was on the verge of reaching terminal velocity as I spun to the bottom. The boat's hull bounced lightly off of the river floor and I got locked into cruising mode. It was very dark but I could still make out shadows from the giant rocks looming around me. I was glad I had a good breath because, with my boat compressed around me, I was neutrally buoyant and there was no sign of me heading for the surface. Finally, with my breath all but exhausted, I went for a Rocket Black Attack for the surface and carped for air on arrival. It was awesome. The next time I hit bottom, I thought I had missed my entrance but hit a second surge in the middle and got pulled down next to the rock in the middle of the river. I bounced off of the rock lightly, then bounced off of the bottom and headed for the surface in the funnel of a large whirlpool.

JIM: Do you have to concentrate on staying cool for real deep Mysteries? Is there a technique for holding your breath so long?

JEFF: The thing I try and think about is relaxing when you get locked in. Once you get into cruising mode (if this happens), you can focus on relaxing and using minimal movements and weight shifts to conserve your energy for a longer ride. If you have to work hard to increase your spin to go deep, you will invariably shorten your fun quotient for that ride (if you are a downtime junkie like me).

JIM: Do you hit the "up button" often? What would make you do that?

JEFF: When you have to resort to using the up button, it is either very good or very bad. Either you have nailed a sweet one and have exhausted your O2 supply, or you have gotten mixed up with some bad charc. I got involved in some bad charc recently at the Sis where, during an entry, my boat was facing downstream with no spin with my bow about head level. I could feel my-self hurling towards the rock in the center of the river and I tried to hit the up button. The damn thing short-circuited and I proceeded to piton straight into the rock which, thankfully, sent me back to the surface. Some-times the up button doesn't work at the Sis like it does in other spots. Most of the time, though, the up button is used for terminating positive events.

JIM: You excel at Mysteries with and without your paddle. If you had to choose one or the other, which would you choose and why?

JEFF: Using a paddle gives you much more leverage to promote flashy exits and do easier transitions. For me, this is fun for a few attempts, but uses up a large portion of my energy. Since I am such a downtime freak, and would rather spend more time on the bottom of the river than on the surface, I conserve my energy for helicopter spins and underwater cruises along the bot-tom of our beautiful Mystery spots. As I mentioned earlier, I find treading is my preferred mode for traveling.

JIM: How much strategy do you use to map out and perform your long Mysteries? What do you concentrate on when you are seeking the depths?

JEFF: Some spots, like Cowbell, have more predictable currents and you can plan for more consistent rides. At Halls and Twisted Sister, each attempt becomes a separate event and you improvise as you go. The thing I try and do consistently is to keep spinning and keep my weight centered over the boat to maintain control.

JIM: How do you use the science of "winging down" while you are trying to sustain a Mystery?

JEFF: I think that is one of the keys to learning to do long, deep Mysteries. Keeping your boat spinning keeps your momentum centered around an axis (your torso) and keeps your weight focused directly over the center of your hull. This is the start to maintaining control on any Mystery Move attempt.

JIM: What advice would you give an intermediate squirt boater who very much wants to achieve big downtime?

JEFF: Pick a spot, tread it, study it, get advice from locals if possible, and work it. It takes time and many, many attempts. At least it did for me.

JIM: Can you describe what your favorite Mystery would be like?

JEFF: It is different in each spot. I know there are many Mystery spots I have not been to, and I am sure every local could tell you his ultimate ride at his spot. My favorite Mystery is every time my head gets wet...

JIM: Is your boat *really* too small?

JEFF: If the boat floats, wear it.

INTERVIEW WITH TRIP KINNEY
(The tall one)

JIM: You've established yourself as a Mystery virtu-oso. Can you describe the lure of the deep?

TRIP: The lure of the deep resides in the portal it provides for an interface with energy. The energy is in the form of the moving water of the river. My passion is to willingly interact with a force that flows with me and past me whether I am there or not. Briefly, my interaction with the river alters the microflow, creating tiny eddies and swirls as I pass and flow with the water. But the macroflow is unchanged. The dance I engage in is with a partner who is wholly indifferent to my antics. Yet, in the ride nothing matters but experiencing the moment. The feeling of being enveloped in the silky murkiness of deep water with tens of thousands of gallons flowing over me and around me is delicious. Gliding, spinning, and looping in this dynamic environment is breathtaking. The deep keeps calling me back because the potential is always there.

JIM: What do you focus on when you roam?

TRIP: The technical aspect of executing a Mystery Move requires thinking about three elements: entrance, down-time, and exit. Initially to get into the deep realm, thoughts of water currents, angle of attack, and energy to access the current are paramount. Once tapped into the seam, thoughts shift to thinking about leveling the hull, underwater currents, positional location for naviga-tion, and establishing a stabilizing spin. On deep rides, these thoughts become background noise. Pressure and darkness are the true measures of location. And of course the occasional terrestrial body in the shape of rocks. The ride consumes all. There is no world up there. There is no stress. There is no me. It is sharp intimacy with an indifferent lover. Finishing the ride can be a slow affair—gentle spiraling back into that world. But it can be desperate—the mind gasping—a hungry return to what is familiar. Returning however quietly, loopily, or gaspingly is best done with intent. The exit should complement the ride and provide a transition from "there" to "back again."

JIM: Do you loop? What's that feel like?

TRIP: Yes, I definitely loop. Loopin' is dynamic!! Loops I remember most vividly are ones done in fast current and Loops done while entering into underwater eddies. The former feels like a roller coaster, the latter like shooting into an eddy amidst turbulent bigwater current. Some days I am a loopin' fool. Looping for the joy of it, for the freedom of the movement. But looping can also be used for boat control to reestablish level after encountering an underwater obstacle.

JIM: Do you open your eyes underwater? How do you map the turf?

TRIP: Almost always I open my eyes underwater. Goggles are an important tool for me with Mystery Moves. I find that goggles help with two dimensions. First, goggles help with maintaining boat level because slight inclinations can be perceived with eyes sometimes before they are felt with hips. Second, goggles help me map the turf. There is nothing like a clear blue-water day with the sun shining through the water. Depending on the Mystery spot it's literally possible to see the eddy walls, to see underwater features, and, yes, occasional underwater denizens. The absence of the ability to see is also important; it often means depth. Mapping the turf is a multi-stage process. Talking to the locals is primary. Locals are the ones to clue me into the most important knowledge, the known danger spots in the riverbed. Seeking the good ride is my responsibility. My approach is to visit a spot at variety of levels including those too low to boat and too high to boat. Swimming around often clues me into a lot about the features. I think playing with entrances can be key to learning a spot's potential. Other variables I key into are light/dark variations, pressure, currents, and rock features. Downtime is the real teacher. It demands that you learn or sends you back to try, try again.

JIM: Where are your favorite sinkspots and what are their perfect levels?

TRIP: My home sinkspot is Cowbell on the Nolichucky River, but I love going into West Virginia to play with the Gauley and New Rivers when I can. As far as perfect levels go, as I develop a relationship with each spot, certain levels speak to me strongest on different days. It depends on the experience I am seeking.

JIM: What does it take for you to hit the up button?

TRIP: Lack of appetite. The up button is more sensitive some days, and less others. I find that the critical factor with the up button is where my appetite is on a given day. It is important to ease into the longer rides. I do this either in my head long before getting to the river through visualizing downtime or by refamiliarizing myself with the feeling of being under with a session or two. Familiarizing can be important in remapping the terrain as well. Hitting the up button is often my mind betraying my flesh into believing that it really needs to expel carbon dioxide. Controlling those false suggestions from the mind requires turning off that persistent (breathe, breathe, breathe) function. Hitting the up button can also be mind complaining that it feels lost and in strange water. My best rides are when I am not scared of where I am going. Every ride has the potential to be superb by tuning in what is important and turning off the distractions.

JIM: What are your feelings about ballasting?

TRIP: Ballasting definitely has its place. My thoughts are if it enhances the fun factor, go for it. If it strengthens the charc, go for it. If it increases the downtime, go for it! Each of us sets the arena for our own experiences. Go with what works.

JIM: You are also an established creeker. What would be a perfect run for you?

TRIP: A perfect run . . . If the Green River (which is dam controlled) had a Mystery spot the equivalent of Cowbell or Twisted at the takeout of the run, that would about do it! My favorite experiences these days are runs that combine exceptional scenic beauty, aesthetic whitewater, and have great water quality. This spring, I had a spectacular day in the Smoky Mountain National Park where I was able to catch a run on the West Prong of the Little Pigeon at juicy flows in my creek boat and then sneak over the ridge to catch a Mystery session on the Little River at the Y in a squirt boat.

JIM: Where did you get those gills?

TRIP: Gurgle, gurgle . . . blub, blub . . .

JIM: What advice would you give to someone who wants to roam?

TRIP: I am still an initiate at roaming. Appetite is the single most important factor I know of. I find that a true desire to roam is paramount. Talking with folks that are experienced with Mysteries and especially about specific Mystery spots has helped me the most. Go spend time at the sinkspots. Get out of your boat and swim, map out the spot, and most importantly, *get down!!!* Be present in that moment, experience the river, and let go. If you want to roam far and deep make sure you develop your appetite. On a technical side . . . I got a custom-made, but most importantly it was a custom-chopped squirt boat. The custom chop makes a huge difference in control. It's a big step (if you're poor) buying a new squirt boat and not one that needs to be made initially. But if you are going to mainline the downtime, it sure makes it smoother.

GLOSSARY OF SQUIRTERMS

Air Blade During a stroke, the paddle blade passing through the air.

Attaining The science of paddling upstream using eddies and seams in currents.

Backblasting Blasting with the bow submerged beneath the foam of a hole.

Back Cut Any squirt move done against the grain or whirlpool alignments.

Backracker A method of exiting holes. A Green Lean applied while facing downstream surfing a hole.

Black Attack A controlled, spinning, vertical exit to a total sub-mersion Mystery Move.

Blast Surfing a slide-type or pourover hole straight on, like a wave.

Boof To impact with the hull. A technique for flat landings from vertical drops.

Bow Squirt To sink a boat's bow in order to set it vertical; a.k.a. Front Pivot.

Cartwheels To flip a kayak end-for-end continuously. Double Enders followed by Smashes.

Charc Charging arc. The angle of attack of a boat's long axis as it encounters local currents/features. Directly related to strategy or lack thereof in river running. A broad charc is perpendicular to the current; a steep charc is toward parallel. Also used in ref-erence to people's attitudes, i.e., bad charc.

Chines Where the sides of the boat meet the bottom of the hull. Hard chine implies a tighter radius of corner than a soft chine.

Chop To reduce the volume of any boat by cutting out material from the seam area.

Chops During Cartwheels, the moment when the portion of the boat that was in the air crashes underwater.

Cluing Blasting performed with the entire boat submerged in the greenwater.

Dense-Boat Theory Small boats perform better than big boats in big water. Counterpoint to the "big water, big boat" theory.

Double Ender After the bow sinks during an Ender or Bow

Squirt, it continues up and out of the water, sinking the stern. Easy half of a Cartwheel.

Duffek To hold a bow draw near the boat. Created by Milo Duffek as a slalom racing technique to turn the boat without slowing it.

Flick A quick backwards spin of the paddle while hunning between strokes.

Freeze Frame To poise absolutely motionless while surfing or running rapids.

Full-Spin Throw A paddle throw where the paddle spins 360 degrees in a plane parallel to the surface of the water.

Future Water The water you will reach at some future moment while riding a kayak that is spinning.

Grain Direction of the flow of the current. Charcs can be with, or against, or even across the grain.

Green Lean A rudder performed by crossing a blade over the stern deck.

Greenwater The portion of a hole that passes below the foam pile; a.k.a. greenwater slab.

Hunning To do a full backwards spin of the paddle between strokes.

Maintained Momentum To keep an end of the boat in motion between moves to facilitate the next move. Essential for a third-point charc.

Meltdown To sink deeply below the foam pile of a hole during a downstream run.

Moonstroking To glide backwards while appearing to paddle forward.

Mush Move Dropping completely underwater on an eddy line, parallel to the grain, on a downstream run.

Mystery Move A Bow and Stern Squirt done in close succession so that both ends of the boat sink completely underwater almost simultaneously. This is an entry technique for whirlpool rides. The reemergence from a complete submersion is called a Black Attack.

Mystery-Smash Up Bow-Screw Double Ender Do a Mystery Move into a Black Attack ending with a Smash Up. From this bow-under position, spin into a Bow Screw finishing with a Double Ender, or even a Screw Up, or a Smash Up if you feel like spicing it up.

Pearling Having one end of the boat dive underwater during a Surf or Blast. Originally developed by ocean surfers wiping out. Usually a lead into an Ender. Sustained pearling is called cluing.

Pepper Pry A Stern Squirt that turns 360 degrees around a single Duffek.

Plow Squirt A Bow Squirt performed by leaning forward and paddling forward.

Rocket Move Leaping from the crest of a wave by doing a Stern Squirt at the base during a downstream run.

Schnitzel To twirl the paddle around one hand and retrieve it.

Screw Up A past vertical Stern Squirt done as a pirouette Backender. A Super Screw Up is a 270-degree spin with a full twist, which feeds you directly back into the eddy. A full-twist 360-degree spin of the bow is a Mega Screw Up.

Shoulders The side structures of a wave. They support the peak.

Shudder Rudder To rudder directly behind the boat while surfing or blasting.

Slo Mo To paddle as if in a slow motion film.

Smash After the stern sinks, this move flips the boat end-for-end so that the bow is under. The tough half of a Cartwheel.

Spacemaker To swing paddle around your head at full arm's length after a Tilla. Describes the minimum required space for squirting to those who are unaware of it.

Splat, Rock A Squirt done in front of or near a rock so the boat passes over or lands on the rock; a.k.a. smears, splatters, pillow squirts.

Splat Scat Gel coat marks left on stones by errant eskimos.

Squeeze An underwater feature of an eddy line. The area where eddy currents are pitted most directly against the downstream currents.

Squirt Sinking all or portions of a boat by using currents and strokes in order to accomplish hot-dog maneuvers.

Squirt Boat A low-volume kayak designed to have little volume above the water in order to facilitate its submersion in the act of squirting.

Stern Squirt A controlled sinking of a boat's stern in order to stand it on end and perform hot-dog maneuvers.

Subbin' Out A Mystery Move exit to a Blast. Clue into a rib and then mystery deeply into the sweet spot. Exit with a Black Attack or Bow Screws.

Supermove A one-handed cross-bow pry performed while crossing an eddy.

Sweet Spot Deadish area in the heart of a foam pile of a hole.

Swipe A Bow Squirt followed by a Double Ender done passing very near a rock. A bow-screw swipe is a bow-screw lead into a swipe exit done passing a swipestone.

Swipestone A stone with good characteristics for accomplishing successful Swipes, i.e., rounded corners and a strong consistent pillow.

Swirl-O-Gram Any lengthy roll in turbulent waters. If rocks are involved, it's a gnarl-o-gram. Go back to "Charc in equals charc out."

Third Point The position of the center of the mass/shape of the boat/rider.

Third-Point Charc The direction of travel of the third point. An imaginary line.

Tilla To roll a paddle over the shoulders and around the neck and retrieve it.

Transition Moves Moves requiring flipping one end of the boat for the other, such as Cartwheels, Smash Ups, and Blasting transitions.

Veer When a kayak establishes an exponentially increasing turning tendency.

Water Blade During a stroke, the portion of the paddle that is in the water.

Wave Move To backender immediately upon exiting a surf.

Weight Throw To control the direction of motion of the upper mass of the boat/rider.

INDEX

ABOUT THE AUTHOR

Jim Snyder has been paddling since 1965 and spent 19 years as a raft guide. He currently makes fine wooden paddles (since 1975) and designs paddles and kayaks (over 60 designs in 20 years). He lives on the banks of the Cheat River in Albright, West Virginia, with his wife Doris and children Nathan and Amelia. Jim helped pioneer the sports of squirt boating and steep creeking. He received the "Legend of Whitewater" award from the American Canoe Association in 1999, and he was selected one of the "Top 100 Paddlers of the Last Century" by *Paddler* magazine. He enjoys winter kayak camping and Thrillseeking steep shallow creeks (ELF boating) as well.

ABOUT THE ILLUSTRATOR

Veteran kayaker W. Nealy (a.k.a. William—not Bill—Nealy) is the well-known author/illustrator of *Kayak, Whitewater Home Companion,* and several popular whitewater humor books.

PHOTOGRAPHY CREDITS

Paul Marshall: pages 37, 38, 48, 52, 61, 62, 80, 88, 114, 119, 123, 132, 167, 190.

Kevin O'Brien: pages 66, 67, 74, 92, 98–99, 106–7, 108, 110, 133, 142, 162, 164, 233.